Terence,
   May the blessings
of light and peace be
yours in the years ahead.
   Sr. Margo

sometimes a star...

m.e. colman

Authors & Artists
Publishers of
New York

Authors & Artists Publishers of New York
3 Kimberly Drive, Suite B
Dryden, New York 13053 USA
www.AAPNY.com

Book Design   Gary Marsden
Cover Design   m.e. colman

Printed in the United States of America

9 8 7 6 5 4 3 2 1

Library of Congress Cataloging-in-Publication Data
Colman, M.E./ Religion/Autobiography

ISBN: 978-0-9787113-2-0

www.MEColman.com

sometimes a star...

Contents

return...

It was several years ago, in the beginning of June. We had just come back from Ireland on one of our trips. Everyone in the group wore that disoriented expression, you know, the unmistakable look portraying the proverbial jet lag inevitably part of the package deal that goes with international travel. Making our way through customs, the baggage carousel was awaiting each of us, adding a sense of vertigo after the long flight. Finally, after retrieving our bags, we said our good-byes, then headed our separate ways.

Driving back home from the airport, thoughts and images of the trip drifted in and out of consciousness... looking out the window of the plane and seeing that beloved, endless green, stretching on for miles like a patchwork quilt, remembering the quality of the light, the sweet fragrance of the air, the sense of time standing still...

Early the following morning, actually during Lauds, a soft voice seemed to come out of nowhere, *"Return... go back and listen to their stories."*

Have you ever had that experience? You know, when you hear a voice inside your head? And it's not the same as hearing voices, to be sure...

All that day, the thought of writing a book was unrelenting. I phoned a few friends over there, sharing with them this idea that would not release me. They were very encouraging, saying they would help in any way they could. On this side of the Pond, donations started coming in for airfare, accommodations, and car rentals. Everything just fell into place.

Countless books and articles about Celtic Spirituality have been published in the last ten to fifteen years. These writings are often inspirational and instructive, yet they refer to days long gone, when legend and fact were enmeshed, lost in the ethereal mists of time. No one is ever sure whether these stories are indeed true! Of course, just using the term "Celts" is going to raise many questions; who were they, where did they originate, where did they go?

Recently, while on another trip to Ireland, we spent our first day in Dublin exploring that wonderful city. We took the time to see the exhibition on the Book of Kells at Trinity College, and visited the Museum of Archeology on Kildare Street. The woman who was assigned as our group guide approached us, drawing me aside. She asked what part of the museum we were interested in seeing, and I responded that we wanted to see some of the Celtic artifacts, the torques, the Ardagh Chalice, and anything else she thought would be relevant to that time period. The woman then informed me that she wanted to make it very clear that she (and most of the well-known scholars in Ireland, according to her) were sure the Celts had never come to Ireland at all. Right, take a moment to think about that!

Nevertheless, this book is really not about the Celts, or Celtic Spirituality, or the past. This book is about you... well, it's about all of us. The questions that were asked of the individuals who appear in these pages are not unlike the questions I ask almost every day, of others, as well as of myself.

All those who shared their thoughts and feelings in the pages that follow are indeed the ones writing the book. Their struggles, their concerns, and their frustrations are so very moving. They speak with an honesty and openness that is almost disarming at times. The floodgates were opened! The outpouring seemed to reflect such incredible trust. It was a humbling experience. These people are all indelibly etched in my memory.

Hopefully you find this book to be meaningful. Perhaps it touches you in ways you had not expected. So much could not be captured on the written page... the unspoken moments, the smiles, the laughter, the joy, the tears, the anger, the love. Consider this as a thank-offering, perhaps a "return" to all those who shared their lives with me.

Perhaps you might think of the book as a collection of portraits, a gallery of "word images"... pinpoints of light, moments frozen in time.

We can see ourselves in these pages as in a mirror. If we take the time to ponder some of the words spoken with such sincerity and truth, we might all be changed, hopefully leading toward healing and transformation.

passionate about what we're at and what we do...

PJ was a man in his mid-forties. Learning more about him in time, it was exhausting just to hear how much he was doing. He had his own small dairy farm, ran a B&B, and managed a nearby food store. He was also a teacher, as well as a father.

"The Church has been so much a part of the Irish culture since way, way back. In fact, it was probably a revolutionary part of the Irish culture in terms that peo-

5

ple looked up to their local priest. He was the leader. And that local community, wherever it was, developed the characteristics of their local pastor, because he was their leader. Very few of them were educated enough to either challenge or ask, 'Is this what we really want or what we really want to do?' So, therefore, many communities in Ireland over the last hundred years would have been products of whatever their local priest was, in terms of character and stature. Some communities were fortunate enough to have very good priests who were great leaders and who had a very broad approach to what community development was about. Other priests would have had a kind of narrow view of what the Church teachings were about, and that also rubbed off. And then sometimes communities just stagnated...

"My experience as a child growing up would be, I s'pose, positive in a sense. When I was a young fella, my mom was in hospital, givin' birth to one of my brothers, and I remember the priest coming daily to my dad to see if he needed to go to the hospital to visit her. Now, this particular priest had a reputation as a no-nonsense operator, from what I can remember, and I always thought how kind it was of him to take time out from his day to come and take my father to visit my mom. So that would have been a positive experience. Then as I grew older, I got involved here in the local community and a youth club. We set up our own youth club. We were around fifteen, sixteen, seventeen. We organized it totally ourselves, without adults, and we developed it quite well. And then one or two people in the community weren't quite happy with the direction we were taking or going, and they got on to a local parish priest at that time, and one night he came and said, 'Here, I'm shuttin' you down.' He had never been to the youth club before—never visited. I was really upset, but I thought that's his personality, that's his style. We just continued on and did our own thing.

"There would have been other encounters—good, some of them very good. As I went through college, I came across a particularly good chaplain, for instance, who I talked to a lot. He loved the country, and I suppose going to college in Dublin, we were two country boys, so we had something in common. Talking to people like that, I would always marvel at people who would sacrifice, what I would consider sacrificing their lives in the pursuit of an ideal. While I wouldn't be prepared to do what they were doing, maybe I sacrifice my life for another ideal, as they would probably see it. But I also

7

admire people who took on that. I remember Fr. Gerry, a Franciscan Father. He came from a large family, like I did. And I remember often talking to him about different perspectives. Some of his family members were so like mine in ways, different characters, and attitudes, and all of that. I always thought, y'know, here was a man who's on a different mission to me, but in many ways, we are the same kind of people. That would have been my college days.

"I often wondered then what the role was of women in the Church. And that really baffled me. As a youngster and a teenager, I questioned everything as I grew up—why could not a woman preach at the altar or go and say Mass? What was wrong with a woman? Certainly there was nothing wrong with my mother. She was able to articulate herself and her points of view. To this day, it's something that I find strange, and I think the Church is missing something by not having the women directly involved. I think that's very welcome in the Protestant churches, where there are women ministers. I think it's a very healthy development. But in the Catholic Church, there is some reluctance. I remember one occasion—a couple of years I was in the States, in New York—a local canon left at sixty years of age to get married. He stood up at the altar one Sunday and said, 'I'm leaving.' The congregation was in absolute shock. The following Sunday, Cardinal O'Connor came out to say Mass and address the audience. He spoke about this man who had gone, but never mentioned his name, which I thought was really sad. I was watching what was going on in the church, and I was watching the antics of the people there. They were all milling around Cardinal O'Connor. And at the end, to me he looked like a pop star with his flock, particularly among the women; they wanted to touch him and shake hands with him. And yet I thought, these people have no real part, they weren't playing any active part in this church. So, bringing that back to an Irish context, I thought it's similar in Ireland in a way. We have very, very good women, but they never get an opportunity to play their active part. OK, right now they are ministers of the Eucharist, and they put the flowers in the church, and make the church look well. I think the priesthood itself would be healthier if there were women priests. That's just my view. If that ever happens, I don't know... but I hope one day it will.

"What I find, a woman's perspective always is different from a man's, and I think that's important for balance. Y'know, the old male clubs... The Catholic

9

Church is probably one of the last remaining male clubs, as such, if you want to call it that. But then again in recent years, there was change, but obviously the present Pope has very definite views about that, and obviously they are very conservative views, so therefore I s'pose it's a challenge that we have to work through. I think it's up to the flock, as we are, to bring about these changes, through discussion, and negotiation, and pointing things out. I think one of the challenges I see the Church having at the moment is the lack of priests because of the very issues that we're talking about—priests cannot marry, there are no women priests allowed. So I think change will be brought about if the Church as an institution is to survive. And that leads on to something else, then... the question of the Church as an institution, or the Church as a spiritual leader. I think there is a dichotomy there of ideas. Usually churches are very rich. And it could be any church, not just the Roman Catholic Church. Now there's nothing wrong with being rich. It's just how you utilize your riches, and how you see everybody within that church, all its members. Are they seen as equal status? Does each of them have an equal status? And sometimes I would venture to say they don't. Like when people are ill, if you have the money to pay for the operation, you can get yours quicker. And if you don't, you have to wait your turn. So, that's the other issue...

"I think the Church spiritually has a very important role to play. Everybody needs spirituality, whether it's contrived or it comes naturally. I think it's important for people to meditate and focus. The Church to me is about getting you to look at yourself, and reflect within yourself what your daily life is about... where you're going and what you're doing. So they're just some of my thoughts..." *(A quick laugh)*

"You're one of the few who's mentioned anything about meditation or spirituality. People don't usually talk about that. There seems to be a holding back from sharing their inner lives..."

"Or is it because they don't ever give themselves a chance? Maybe they don't have those kinds of words. I think it's a question of words. The Irish might be shy of putting words on things. They would maybe feel all those things, but they would call it something else, maybe. They might call it prayer, and prayer seems very informal, as such. But I think everybody reflects, every

11

day of their lives, but it's a question of how you label what you're doing. Like when you come in from the field at night, or come in from your work in the day, you reflect back over your day, and you think, 'Maybe tomorrow I'll do that differently, or I'll make a change there.' That's basically meditating about what you're doing. And then there's the inner meditation of yourself as well. Particularly nowadays, people seem to have more and more leisure, they want more and more leisure. I think it's important that people take time out for them-selves. People say to me, 'You're very busy all the time.' A lot of the times when I'm at my busiest, I'm meditat-ing, my mind is somewhere else as well. I'm relaxed, I'm thinking about what I'm doing, and I'll see a spiri-tual side of it at times. Sometimes I find in some of my work, it's inspirational in terms of what I do, and I feel that inspiration is coming from, from, uh, from some-where else. Sometimes you make decisions, and you make decisions in the dark, and they all seem to work out, most times, anyway. And you think, 'That was a good idea,' and that idea came from somewhere. So, you have to allow yourself to be open to change. I think it's the great challenge for us, to be able to cope with the change in faith. I was reading somewhere recently that we are in the age of creativity, which we are very much. The age of prophecy is over, and the age of technology is here, but where the real challenge is now is in the age of creativity, being creative. If people want to become millionaires, to be very rich, they must look at this and say, 'If we want to become rich in our lives, we have to become creative for ourselves.'

"As for me, I am happy as a peacock. You could say to me, 'You should go away for a weekend.' But I'm happiest when I'm sittin' at home in my own house. To me, this is my space, and I find it so relaxing. I could go to America, which I do very often, to New York. And I go to Europe, to Germany. But to spend a Sunday evening here, or any day... just to sit down and relax for a couple of hours, to me, that's heaven, because it's my space and I am happiest here.

"Getting back to the Church... In recent years I have come across two very good priests. I've come across some very ordinary priests, but there have been two very exceptional priests. One of whom was here in the parish, who actually previously owned this house, and the other was in a neighboring parish. Both elderly men. It always fascinated me. One had tremendous energy, the chap who was here. Tremendous energy, doing things always.

13

Every time you'd meet him, he was thinking of a new idea, either for the parish or for something else. And if he wasn't thinking of the parish, he'd be suggesting something to you that you should be doing. To me, that's the Gospel alive, that's the living Gospel. Because you can read Scripture, you can read from the books, but... Most people, when they go to church on Sunday, they go there out of a sense of obligation. And also if they don't go, their neighbors will know that they're not going, and the word will get around: 'Well, Jack is not going to Mass, what's wrong...' and, 'They're not good people any more.' And Jack might have had a rough day at home. That's just one perspective.

"Fr. Thomas, who was here—the one with tremendous energy—to me, he was the living Gospel. Then the other priest was called Fr. Willie. He told us one time, when he was a young priest, the bishop put him into a convent to be chaplain to nuns. And for eight years of his life, as he said to us, what a waste of a young man's life. And that was the thinking years ago in the church. I loved going to hear Fr. Thomas, his homilies. Just to hear him speak, because he spoke about the community—what they were doing that week, what happened in the community—and he translated it into what the

Gospel was about. We would stop and joke with each other after Mass, and he'd say, 'Well, you didn't get mentioned today, you mustn't have been doin' anything right this week.' People were talking about it in a very positive way, I think. They saw a funny side, but he was getting them to talk about it, and you knew he was reaching them because they were talking about it afterwards.

"Then other priests come, like they're just pure theologians, as such, who don't have any relationship to the local community. I think if you're in any group of people, you have to be able to relate, that's the key to it. You have to be able to relate to the people that you're with. If you don't relate, you're going to become isolated very quickly. And I think that is what has happened, in some ways, in the Church. There is a drive on, a renewal... parish renewals, and activities like that. But it takes time. I think it's incumbent on priests now; they have to be out in the community, doing things. It's more and more difficult. Now it's more challenging, because they really have to work at it. Before, they could dictate... and preach. Now they have to speak with people. That is the challenge.

"I guess in Ireland—being a Celtic country and the Celtic blood—we are very complex and adverse in our thinking at times. We are often very passionate about what we're at and what we do. Change is always slow, I think. Even though change can be very rapid sometimes, I s'pose, we are slow and we resist change very much because of our nature. Whereas in a place like the States, it's much more of a melting pot, and you learn how to tolerate each other much more quickly, because you have no choice. The numbers are against you, so you have to learn how to tolerate. Whereas here, we are all very alike in many ways. Basically, we are all Christian. Frankly, everybody's way of thinking is Christian. There might be small divergences, but it's basically Christian. So, there are some of the challenges."

"What is really meant... what would you say is Celtic?"

"One of the characteristics, of course, is the passion. The Celts would have been warriors, as such, and also would have been pioneers. As I would define it, they were a collection of Europeans who moved towards the West. They would be very family-oriented—community-oriented—and very passionate. I s'pose the challenges they encountered and the energy it took to overcome these challenges, it was physical, it was mostly physical, in terms of moving into a place like Ireland of years ago and living in the country."

"When people speak of the Celtic Spirit, passion may indeed be part of it. What are some of the other characteristics?"

"Paganism. Y'see, they would've worshipped their own gods. And nature was very much a part of that, they were very close to nature, and the elements of nature."

"The Roman influence, the liturgy and the doctrines... it seems to be incongruous with the closeness to nature, and this passion you speak of. One woman went as far as to say that in some ways she feels the Roman Church has tried to suppress your Celtic roots. Some people have said, perhaps twenty years from now, they're wondering if maybe the churches will be empty."

"Well, again, that comes back to the point about the local priest, what he does to engage his flock. He won't engage them any more by talking at 'em, or talking to them. He has to be out among them. People will have to decide whether to see the Church as a place to go and reflect and meditate on their weekly lives and on their daily life, or not. And if not, then the churches will be empty. No longer can we say, 'Well, the Great Commandment... you commit a sin.' I think it's much more than just words for people. It has to be a feeling of expression for people and the community's spirit of that, where they're going, and reflecting on it. People won't take anybody's word. They have to feel it for themselves, because they have choices now. Before, people had no choice. To get out to their church on Sunday was a very social thing to do. Now people are out every other day, and they don't have to go to church to socialize. So, I think the Church will take on a new meaning and it will bring new challenges as well, in terms of where it's going to go and the direction it will take. It's a great place to be. I think some bishops are realizing that. Our bishop, I think, is realizing that. He is someone who would be quite open about how he sees the Church's role in our life. There was no place in the Church years ago for people who were separated and divorced. Now that's accepted. There was no place in the church for people who, let's say, who were unmarried. And that has changed. It's changing... slowly. And maybe the slower

18

change is better. It's more concrete."

"What about the economic boom here in Ireland in recent years, the so-called Celtic Tiger, and how that's affecting people?"

"I think what happens there, how I would see that happening is... The economy is going well at the moment. But everything is cyclical. And also peoples' lives are cyclical. When I was a youngster, a young teenager growing up, at that stage, none of my friends had any great difficulties. They all were from different homes; their parents were alive. But as you move on through life, you came across maybe one or two who lose their parents, you might lose a brother or a sister, through illness, through accidents. Community is the same way. It will lose members. And it brings home the reality that we need the support of people, and to support each other. And it's through these experiences—and I've watched this over the years, it's true—that people realize how much they need each other through these times. Because when you're young, and especially if you have money, I s'pose, you feel like a tiger. Nothing can touch you.

"Life is very fickle, very fragile. The challenges of

19

life are bound to take their toll. People suddenly realize the needs of their lives, and spirituality is part of that. I s'pose one of the things that's happened now, and people talk about it a lot, sayin', 'People are moving to other religions.' That's judgment. All the people are doing is finding a new way to express themselves. They may be doing it through a new medium; maybe they're just finding another way that they can identify with.

"So the Tiger, going back to your earlier question. He has maybe pushed things quicker economically, but spirituality has nothing to do with it, in a sense. I'm not sure if that makes any sense to you?"

"Is the Celtic Tiger going to affect people in their seeking a deeper kind of spirituality?"

"I think the danger there is people may not take time because they are so busy, and that goes back to the beginning of our talk, taking time to meditate and reflect. People are so caught up in the world, family life, making ends meet. Because people take on more and more in terms of work, and there are more demands in their life... to be successful. Then there's a price to be paid for that. I think, inevitably, people will return to their spirituality. Because they'll have to! They'll need it.

"If everybody was on a plane, and told the plane was going down, they would very quickly have a conversion back to where they came from. Their roots would really come through very quickly. We're fine when we don't need help, but when we need help, we very quickly call for it."

"So true... when we're in crisis."

"Yeah, when we're in crisis, we'll very quickly call for it."

Sometimes a Star…

we can't survive
without one another...

Monica was a woman in her mid-sixties. She was very articulate, with a quick laugh that followed many of her thoughts and words. Our "chat" took place in a public garden. It was a beautiful day, with many others walking slowly around, apparently just enjoying the weather and the setting. While we sat on the slope, the sound of a small stream could be heard, gently rippling down the hillside. She started right in, seemingly eager to speak...

"...lot of emphasis has gone on the physical side of life, not on the spirit life. Many won't go to religious

23

functions, or whatever. But I think it's human nature, anyway. It's like fashion! It swings around. It comes around. Mind you, they're more serious subjects... religion, and the life of the soul and the hereafter." *(Pause.)* "But with this research now, would you... um, this surely will lead you into examining more of the teaching, surely, of your Mother Church, if you like... its teachings and why all these changes..."

"I guess the motivation for why I am doing this project is because after coming here many times, I began to notice that there seemed to be such a gap between many of these books that are being written on Celtic Spirituality, and what I was seeing while here. So I was actually led—I believe this is all God-led, Spirit-led—to return and listen to people's stories and find out what is their relationship with the Church, where they find God, what sustains them. These are the kind of questions that I ask. Now, what I've been finding is that some people, especially in their fifties and sixties and older, are saying—and I remember my mom's stories too—that back in their childhood, things were really rather strict. I've seen quite a bit of anger directed toward those years..."

"Oh, not so, not so! I look back on the days that we would go to 9 o'clock Mass... back then, the school children's Mass was 9 o'clock Mass. The girls would sit on the right, and the boys on the left, and we would sing the Kyrie. I remember when we would go to what we called a High Mass, the Feast of Christ the King was one of those days. Sundays we would have a High Mass. I remember the Bishop had a little candle in a little candle holder. And of course 'twas all symbolism, and you would see in some of the children's faces. You know the story 'The Beauty and the Beast' that they portray now in cartoon form? But no, I look back, and it was also a social, it was also a social outlet. No, I never, never felt that I was forced to go at all. As I said, it was a social outlet. Used to love the singing, and enjoyed it. On a Sunday night, we had Compline. We used to go to Compline. And you see, I don't think people went because they had to go. I think they liked going. And we used to have Confraternity on a Monday night and a Tuesday night. Monday night was the men's night. Tuesday night was the women's night. And we'd have standards of saints, y'know, they were there. Tisn't long that they're gone now from the Cathedral, actually, but they had to be removed. They used to be down by the

Baptismal Font. They were secured there against the wall.

"But you went in there, into church... You see, 'twas a way we met people, we met family relations and we met people we knew. And we had a common aim. I can't remember the exact format, but there would be Benediction and there would be certain prayers. And of course the Compline; loved singing the Compline. No, no, looking back to childhood, my religion was a very happy time, never felt forced at all. But the challenge is more now, actually, than it was back in those years. I think the challenge comes more later in life, especially with the changes. One feels, even in the secular world, things have been taken away from us even within our town now. We have no cinema, we've no place of entertainment, except the public house, which we don't all want to go to. People go there very often because they're lonely and they want to drown their sorrows. We have no common venue where we could meet spontaneously. You'd meet, for instance, at the cinema. People would follow a certain film star, and you'd know that you would meet them there. It just took you out of your ordinary, mundane world. The same in the dance hall. All age groups were there, all age groups were there...

26

(And she continued, almost without taking a breath!) "I think today adults must—well, I s'pose 'must' is a strong word—but if they would look at religion now as adults. One is tempted to say, 'Oh, what's the point, everything is gone astray.' But who's to say? I'd be the loser if I was to give up practicing my religion because of some hurt or some disagreement or whatever. But you see, basically everything is still the same. The doctrine is still the same. It's the application of the doctrine that's changed. But 'twas the lead-up to that, the preparation for people. It all came about so quickly. And I just think they weren't prepared for it. It will bear fruit in time. We will be people who will think for ourselves. I don't think I ever went to Mass because the priest said so or because there was a certain priest saying Mass, or whatever. I would go because I wanted to go. The same now, same now... no matter what they would do, no matter who did what. It wouldn't matter to me. I think the Lord is showing us now that we're all human. We're all very human. Perhaps, even if a person has a professional life—a teacher, or a doctor, or something like that—if they fall, we just crucify them. Because we equate being educated, and having had opportunities of developing spiritually and all these things, with the fact

that you can't go wrong, because you have all this knowledge, and you've had all this spirituality, so you should never fall. And I think that's what happened. That, 'Oh, my...' Even in Britain, if a Minister, if something happens, 'Oh, look what they've done,' y'know. And we mustn't forget, I think the Lord is showing us that they're vulnerable as much as we are... perhaps more vulnerable. After all, they have dedicated years of study—they've given years to study—to prepare to serve people. They initially set out to serve people... and things just maybe went astray. Because they're human beings! But the Church still goes on, because Christ said, Christ said, that the Church will go on. The gates of Hell will not prevail against it. It will still survive, no matter what happens. And I think again, reading Church history would be great for adults, y'know, to get everything in perspective."

"Yes, a sense of continuity..."

"Yes, and that the present is a result of the past. All that happened in the past was a preparation for all that's happening now. I think we have to look at history, the past, to understand the present better. One wonders if

Pope John XXIII had lived a bit longer to realize the Holy Spirit is leading the Church. For instance, you take—in the world, in the secular world—you take the great physicist, Stephen Hawking. Look at him. He's so disabled. But he's going on with his work, of exploring the universe and showing it to the world. You could parallel, could you not, parallel those two? Even though he's so disabled and he's using modern machinery communicators to continue because he loves that work so much. And he wants people to know what, what... what wonders there are out there. And you could parallel it with, um, spirituality, then."

(She continued, without hesitation.) "But the Church will never force you or say, 'You must go do this or that.' The thing is, if you join a club, you have to observe certain rules and regulations. You can bring an outsider in with permission. There's always legislation in these things. I don't know whether it was a good analogy or not, because one is spiritual, the other isn't. But within the Church, if you wish to belong to a particular religion, and be a practicing member of it, well, these are the rules and regulations. It is said that to be a good Catholic is very difficult. Well, to be a good Christian today is very difficult—Christian, Catholic. Catholic, of

29

course, 'tis actually Christianity, but it's Catholic because... well, it's open to everybody. From that point of view, it's Catholic, because it's open to every creed in the world... sorry, every, every person in the world, rich, poor, or whatever. It's open to everybody. The door isn't shut on anyone. But it has to come from them. Nobody's allowed to enter unless they really show that they wish to belong to the Church, that nobody has coerced them in any way to become a Catholic, to enter the Catholic Church. And they go through a process. I think the converts have this marvelous advantage over born-into-the-religion Catholics. They go through the process of religious instruction, and they go through the process of becoming a catacumenist and then having the Baptism on Easter Sunday at the Vigil Mass, the Vigil Mass on Easter Sunday. Again, it's goin' back to what it would have been in the past. That's what it would have been in the past..."

"We were talking before about what I noticed was a vast difference between the books that are written on Celtic Spirituality and..."

"I haven't read them now, so I can't make any comment on them."

"...and what's really going on in Ireland today. A lot of the books are written about, well, the Celtic roots and that sort of thing."

"I s'pose if we were to look at those, they go back to pagan Ireland of years ago!"

"Some of them do! And yet, if you talk with some people, they agree that, well, the love of music, for instance, and poetry, closeness to nature, the need for community..."

"These are all universal now, and that's coming to the fore more and more, that people do need to have to belong to a community, and feel they belong to a community. And yet, at the same time, we are cutting ourselves off. In the past, there were all these rows of houses built, except in the countryside. But in towns, there were all these rows. Of course, now they wish to be separated, individual. That appears to be the scene now, for some, some... It's not always possible, people haven't the money, to buy land and live exclusively to themselves, or semi-exclusively to themselves. But it's of our nature that we have to be communal and that we have to share. We can't survive without one another. So therefore, it's bound to come back. 'Twill come back. 'Twill take its time, but 'twill come back, maybe in a different form. I don't know…"

"What about the young people today? A lot of them seem to drift away, not wanting to go to church. Is there a concern there? What can you say to that?"

"Yes, there's a certain concern, but… it's only the Holy Spirit can bring them back, and we setting example by our lives. They do look to adults. You must live what you say, they believe. But we're fallible, and although we say we'd be such and such, we will maybe fall by the wayside, but nevertheless, I think they have to look to Christ, and I think that nobody can force them at all. They'll come back with the Holy Spirit, I'd say, in their own way... I was very surprised; I was up at the University in Cork on Ash Wednesday, and the amount of students going around with their ashes on their forehead. There's a church up there, 'tis quite big, the University Chapel, and they were queued out beyond the doorway, waiting for ashes. So they're expressing it in a different way, they're expressing it in a different way. But, uh... time, only time will tell. The Holy Spirit will lead them back to the Sacraments, the life of the Church, in that respect... but in time." *(Pausing, then speaking very quickly:)* "Well, I think there's more of a challenge for the older generation than the younger generation because the younger ones can't compare—we can! You know, a lot has changed that we grew up with. We have to sort of re-establish ourselves, I s'pose, re-find ourselves to a certain extent. Probably many hold on to their, um... certainly their beliefs of the past, and devotional exercises. But there's a contradiction in that, 'tis amazing, as I say, some Catholics will go over to these religions that are very ascetical, and they're asked to do things. For instance, they wear patches on their nose and shave their hair. If they were asked to do something like that within the Catholic Church, they'd fly out the door! They wouldn't do it! We're not asked to do it, it's put there to us. This is what is to be... And of course the Commandments, the Ten Commandments are for everybody, the whole of the human race. But within the Catholic Church, the regulations for receiving the Sacraments, and the Doctrine and that, I think this is why people have actually entered the Catholic Church. Politicians, and people of note, they've entered the Catholic Church because they see that so many things are unchanging. There's a rock there to hold on to; in the Sacraments, in the teaching on marriage, and abortion and so on. Ya see, there's a stability in that. The Sacraments, for instance, one time Latin would be the everyday language. But at the time of the Apostles, 'twas Aramaic, or Hebrew, or whatever language the people spoke. So going into the vernacular is nothing unusual. It was always there. Everything was in Latin because it was the language of the time. There was a mysticism about it. We knew what we were saying, and we knew what we were singing, in our hymns and canticles and all that. In the Mass, we used to have the corresponding translation in our missals, with the Latin and the English. I never found it any difficulty at all. But there was certainly a mysticism and mystery about the whole thing. But isn't it wonderful now that it is in our own language? And it is nothing unusual, because it would have always been like that. There would have been the participation of the lay people. That must have happened in the early church, it would have happened, because the lay people used to take the Eucharist to other Christians.

When they were in prison, they'd some way or the other get it through to them. Now we have the Eucharistic ministers. So, if you like, there's nothing new under the sun. Things are just recycling, I think. That's the way I see it, anyway. I'm still learning, as one always is, I s'pose. You go on learning, and looking, and seeing things..."

"If I may ask, what sustains you?"

"For instance, if I was facing difficulty?"

"Yes, or just ordinary, day to day."

"Oh, the belief that God is there, and that putting things in His Hands couldn't be safer than in His hands. We have to do a certain amount ourselves. He has given us an intelligence to apply it where it need be. But where it's beyond us then, or beyond me, we need to give it to God. And that's what my mother, and my family did, too. Put it in God's hands. When you can do nothing else, what is there? What is there? And that keeps one sane, it keeps one... I mean, what else? Again, believing there is a higher force, that there is a God. And leave it in His hands, insofar as one isn't able to do anything further for oneself. That's the way I would see it."

(Pause)

"What are your hopes?"

"Oh, that the Church will revive. It will. It will. It will take its course. But human beings, we're very fickle, we're very complex. I would see going to Mass as a time of going to thank. And to place—which is the offertory—to place one's family, one's cares, the world if you like, on the altar. Again, putting everything on the altar. For instance, one hears of these tragedies in the world. It's very difficult to look at these things. And why it's so difficult is because you're so totally helpless to do anything to help these people. So, one prays that those who are in a position to help will help. And one helps insofar as giving a donation, to inspire those who have the ability, the money, the means of some kind or another, that they would go forward and help.

"There is a lot of unseen good going on. And where there is that unseen good, people don't often speak about what they do. They see it as nothing. They don't see it as

36

they're doing marvelous things. They would see all that is needed to be done, rather than what they have done. That's the way it seems to me.

"And how grateful we should be to have this peace and quiet here where we are sitting in this garden. And yet there are so many, flooded out of their homes, or after an earthquake, or whatever—we just can't comprehend it—families not knowing where the others are, whether they're dead or alive after a natural disaster

"This is heaven. There's nothing like that here... nothing like that here. And in a lot of places around the world, there's that security. But some parts of the world seem to be getting it more [*adversity*].

"And of course, we of ourselves can't do the whole thing. It has to be a chain, hasn't it? It has to be a chain. And to look for the truth, to look for the truth in everything, that's the thing... to find the truth, and ask for the grace to follow that truth. But I'd say, no matter what, I would still believe in the Church and carry on. Surely, there are some failings in one form or another, but there have been in the past. As I say, the little bit of church history I've heard or read... surely things have always been the same. There are really marvelous things happening now, in the secular world and in the spiritual world as well. But again, we're up against... there're two spiritu-al worlds, aren't there? I needn't tell you!   And I'd say perhaps young people aren't aware of that, I dunno, how many people would be aware of that? But this is it... and casting, sowing seeds of doubt is the great way of... And pessimism. Pessimism is the way that the Enemy of All Good tries to win, isn't it? Isn't it? Seeds of doubt, and pessimism... and hopelessness, and helplessness, I think. But does that answer...?"

"That speaks very much to what I am seeking... some of the answers. And, of course, your perspective. Everybody has a different perspective. So yours was very much needed, just like everyone else's is."

(After a few moments, Monica continued, with almost a wistful tone in her voice.)

"I haven't been up here now in a long time. I haven't been here in a long time. I haven't been in these gardens at all..." *(Looking at the tiny stream nearby)* "That's a natural spring."

"Yes, isn't it lovely?"

"With the hills here, we have a lot, of course. We used to have one out at the countryside, down at the side of the road. But that's gone now... that's gone now. I'd say this one was always here, must have always been here. Is it going in there, recycling the water? Otherwise 'twould become very stagnant. At one time, actually, they parted these grounds for those who were unemployed—the Sisters of Mercy allowed them to grow their vegetables here..."

(Monica took a few moments of reflection, and went on...)

"I think we're all inse— You see, we say the Church... we're all the Church. It's the administrative side, and there's the laity, you see. But we're all the Church, and we're all searching, no matter what our role in the church—in administration, or whatever. And as I say, they dedicated their years of study and youth to set out to, to... spread the Word of God. I think they have to be given credit for that. And I think that it's just a phase again the Church is going through. We have to see, y'know, how we find our way through it, and come out. We will come out triumphant in the end because Christ is with the Church. Christ is with the Church through the end. Is it the Old Testament, where God was in the breeze? We expect oh, absolutely storming and vibrant, but 'tis quiet. So that's the way He seems to work. That's the way He seems to work... and anything worth getting isn't easy to get. As I say, to investigate our religion as adults—we learned it as children—but to investigate it as adults, and to reflect on how we're living it and so on, and how we can live it to the best of our ability. Basically, isn't that what it's all about? Irrespective of what another is doing... Now it is helpful, 'tis inspiring to see somebody... I've been inspired by people who've been through very hard times, and they've come through in the end, y'know, they've come through it through their faith, and they have overcome great sorrow and everything. And that gives another great strength. Well, if the Lord helped them to do it, He can help me to do it! It's inspiring from that point of view of learning from another. That's why the saints are there... to, to imitate. And they're not canonized saints unless it's possible to imitate their lifestyle. Therese of Lisieux... they said, 'What would we write about her when she died? There's nothing we can write about

40

her...' Did you not know that?"

"I never knew that story... 'there's nothing we can write about her...' Unbelievable."

"All she did was put up with the tedium. She wasn't well, and wasn't able to follow the severe rules of the convent, because of her bad health. I don't think she had to rise as early in the morning. She fell asleep during a meditation, seemingly... and when she woke up, she said, 'Well, the Lord loves his children asleep as much as awake'." *(Quick laugh.)* "And of course, her model was St. Teresa of Avila. Her name was the French version of Teresa, Teresa of Avila... she is marvelous, Teresa of Avila. When she was reforming the order..." *(Speaking very quickly:)* "Mind you, I think in hearing and reading some of the things that happened in the past, if they happened now, I don't know what we'd do!" *(Quick laughter again.)* "Oh my goodness, those medieval times... goodness, gracious me... there's no comparison at all. But Teresa was trying to reform the Church. And St John of the Cross ended up in prison as a result. There's a story, when she was goin' across a river or somethin'. She fell and twisted her ankle, and she

41

said, 'Lord, no wonder you have so few friends if this is the way you treat them!' And you just wonder, what these great people have said, giving out to the Lord, as it were. She felt confident that she could give out to the Lord, because she knew He would love her just the same, as Therese did, asleep—that He loved her just as much, falling asleep—because she wasn't well and being up early hours of the morning like that. He loved His children asleep as much as awake. I think 'tis very encouraging, very encouraging."

"But both those stories seem to indicate a close relationship with God; a very intimate relationship, almost a friendship."

"Oh, yes... and understanding, because friends can't speak to one another like that either, unless there is that, can they? In ordinary, everyday life, a true friend, they say, is someone who knows your faults and loves you just the same. There's another lovely story... A child is standing on a wall or somewhere. It seems very high up. And the father says, 'Jump!' Puts his arms out, and the child isn't a bit worried because the child knows that the father's goin' to catch him when he jumps. I don't know that there's danger there, if there's a fire or something. There's some instance, anyway, where the child knows that the father is goin' to catch him. And you see that in everyday life, with children. The father will be with a small child, a small toddler, and the child will be laughing away. The child knows the feel of the father and is secure. That's what our life should be with God. He won't let us down.... y'know, that he'll always be there. But we have to do our bit too, we have to do our little bit, too."

"But y'know, part of doing that little bit is..."

"Maybe it's a big bit!" *(Laughter.)*

"Yes! But to really go to that place within each of us that is somewhat like the child... it's so difficult."

"Yes, to be child-like, not child-*ish*. And that's something we get mixed up in... child-like, no matter how old we are..."

"That wonderful abandon and trust of a child."

43

"That was St. Therese's, St. Therese of Lisieux, that was her motto, abandonment to God. Abandon, as she called it. She put up with the annoyances, the everyday annoyances. But again, another then is asked to follow in a different way. We're not all able to do that!" *(Laughter.)* "That was her way to the Lord, and that it is possible—even in the smallest ways—to find very close friendship with God…" *(Pause.)* "Well, there we are. So I hope that will help…"

"Yes, it will. Thank you so much for your time! I know you are very busy."

"…and the positive side. We're all searching, no matter what our role is within the Church, within the world…"

"Well, this will be a counterpart…"

"And what's marvelous today is that there are people… they are searching. They are searching. A program like Oprah Winfrey now, she shows that. And she always has a spot in it, depending on the program. If it's something where people have difficulties and that, she has 'life in the Spirit.' It's a little bit she has before the end of the program. And as she says, whatever that Spirit is that you believe it to be. Of course she's going out to people who have no religion, no belief in the hereafter, whatever... And she's a woman who has suffered. And through her suffering, she's come to this, she's come to this..."

(A short, reflective moment, then she continued.)

"I think, too, that... I think at one time there, the Church was a bit nervous of humanism taking over. I remember one time... was it a church in Liverpool? At the time of the Vietnamese War, during or after it, they had photos from the newspapers and that, underneath the Way of the Cross—you know we have the Way of the Cross. I mean, when you think of that...

"If we saw a young man now in the town who had done nothing but good in the town, and this rogue, then... We were asked to make a choice who would be released from prison. That's what happened, with Jesus. And this man who was going about doing good... they saw Him only as a man, they didn't see Him as the Son

45

of God, the ordinary, everyday people. Even though he probably healed them, or gave sight to them, whatever… They flocked after him and couldn't see enough of him, and listened to Him, and were blessed by Him and had their children blessed by Him, and then they turned around and they… But of course it was the custom, the thing that I don't think people realize, the way he was punished was the custom of the day, y'know, that he was lashed… and, of course, the crowning of thorns—that was the idea of the guards—and being crucified. If that happened today, I don't know what we would think at all.

"But I was going to say something else. I forgot now… I've gotten off onto Christ… Again, doing good… I mean, just take Mother Teresa. Terrible things were said about her, that she was doing it for notice. If the Master suffered that way, then the followers are bound to suffer as well, if you're trying to reach out, to bring healing and peace. It's human nature… there will be misunderstandings. So, again, although we're going a lot into reflection… Are we lacking reflection today? And we take a lot of things on hearsay, instead of investigating or analyzing ourselves… because so-and-so said it. Yes, it's true… and yet things that did happen that are a fact, we don't believe 'em. Back to the Master in the end... what he did...

"We have a free will. On television recently, there was a study where they're praying for a group of people who are ill, and another group who are ill but they're not praying for them. A scientific thing, really, more than the spiritual. They're saying, 'Well, God didn't help all those people who were lost or suffered in natural disasters.' A lot of good comes out of these things. God will get good out of anything, will draw good out of it. But we have a *free* will. The universe is made in such a way and will go a certain way... The elements are something that will really bring us to our knees. We are defenseless against the elements. Who was telling me recently... Oh, yes, there was a landslide, and a person had a statue of Our Lady of Lourdes on her windowsill. She would have been about two houses up from where it happened, and she was never touched or affected by it. Her house wasn't touched. She maintains that Our Lady was looking after her. And the same with the loved ones who have left us, surely... they left us in this world. Even if because of their upbringing or because of their own temperament or whatever, they haven't been as good as they should have been. They will try to surely make up for

47

that, I think, in the next world...in the next world. Again, life is a mystery, from beginning to end. And we just have to search for the truth, and try to follow it and try to help one another..."

At this point, a few ladies approached and addressed us with the customary salutations: "Hullo, ladies, isn't it a gorgeous day! Absolutely gorgeous..."

I thanked Monica for her time and we walked up the hill toward the parking lot.

my vision of the future...

Tim was a young priest in his early thirties. We first met at the Rock of Cashel when a concert of Liam Lawton's music was being performed. Tim was very personable and seemed to enjoy the interchange of our dialogue together. The usual questions were presented, asking him to say something about himself, where did he find God, what sustained him...

"When I was eight or nine, I began piano lessons..."

"Oh, you play the keyboard? I knew you sang..."

"No, I mainly play the organ and piano. But, actually, sometimes I feel more at home playing piano. Maybe it has something to do with confidence, your kind of 'behind' instrument, or whatever. It's only in the last two years that I've started singing with Liam in concerts. I found it very frightening, initially, standing out there. For the first few concerts, I would look shocking, frankly. The conductor said, 'You're goin' to have to do somethin'.' I can see him now. He does this *(making a facial gesture)*—the audience can't see him—and all of a sudden everyone in the choir smiles. I find it very hard to remember that I was communicating with my face, 'cause I'm not at home, standing way out there, singing.

"I s'pose the life on the hill, the lifestyle, gives me a lot of quiet time. I don't have to look for it on my own. So, if I could think, 'Do I need quiet time?' then I would say, 'No, I don't,' but my life is kinda quiet sometimes. I also like the buzz and the energy, but even after holiday, I find it very difficult to come back. I do a lot of these weddings. I find that as a priest for weddings, you're kinda keeping it all together. You're like a manager. You're goin' after all these people, and inside I'll not be there. And at a funeral and all that... I have one tomorrow and one Saturday. After a while I get into it, but I s'pose in one sense, I am an introvert. And why am

I a priest, because a lot of it is extroverted—meetings and standing up and talking? So, um, that's difficult. But it has helped my confidence, I think, all these concerts and stuff...

"In secondary school, there was a priest in our parish that I looked up to. He was very dynamic. I was very involved with music—church music—at a young age. I think I was only around thirteen. So I was learning all these new songs, and other choirs were coming to hear us. There was new music being written. I admired him and he was very dynamic. He was friendly with our family, too. But looking back now, I would say that if I had my life to live over again, I wouldn't have become a priest so young. I went to seminary when I was nineteen. There were seventy in our class. And out of those seventy, there were about twenty-five who stayed. And out of two hundred and fifty clerics, now there are maybe a hundred and thirty? Sometimes I question why I'm still here, and I say, 'Oh, that's normal.' I think I am getting more confident with not feeling happy all the time, or not feeling comfortable about whether I should be a priest or not, 'cause I think I am realizing that this is... normal for me. But I think everyone feels like that about their way of life, whether it's marriage, or religious life,

51

single life, whatever… I think what gives me confidence and keeps me going is maybe when God kinda says, 'Look, I want you to be there.' And I s'pose I get affirmation from things I am involved in—funerals, weddings, liturgies, or singing or music—then I say, 'This is why I am here.' So maybe in the boring times, then, you just have to go through those, 'cause that's just life...

"Y'know, in a way I find preaching is not my thing, but sometimes I wonder maybe it is. Goin' back to what you said about being an introvert and talking… I find it very hard to talk, to ad lib, at Mass. I don't think in seven years I've ever stood up—and I think I've only done it once or twice—without having a text in front of me. Now what does that say? I s'pose I'm saying I need a safety net, or I don't have the confidence. But also I wouldn't have the confidence, that I wouldn't be able to think things through and say things, and not say, 'Oh, I didn't mean to say that.' 'Cause I always feel it's a very privileged, and yet a dangerous kind of thing, preaching. You have this captive audience. They're not goin' to disagree with you, unfortunately, to be sure. You're standing up there… and I hate it when a priest will go on and on pontificating. I don't want to do that. That's why I prepare it and I always type it out. I know it's supposed to be the spoken word, not the written word, but hopefully I type it as if it's spoken.

But that night I was thinking... 'Oh, preachin', I don't want to preach.' So I just came up with this thing about the building at Cashel and that the Church is not the buildings. Thinking of all that history that night, this Rock is so important. And at the time I'm sure people were going around saying, 'This place will never cease to exist.' And we were in the ruins. So, I think it was a sobering thought for me 'cause I was thinking... cathedrals and all the property the Church has and all the energy we put into minding it, insurance and money and headaches. And like, we can't see its future. It might be a ruin, it might be a hotel, or something else. I think that's why I said what I did that night, 'cause for me the Church is never a building. So I think I was speaking from my heart that night."

(Tim paused, as if waiting for a prompt.)

"Something we were talking about before... Oh, hopefulness. One of the other priests I spoke with seemed so tired, maybe burned out. You said you didn't want to lose hope..."

53

"Maybe it's a human thing. Is it about being young, being younger? I think it's easy to be more like this when you're young. I've seen priests and nuns who kind of struggled and lived so many years, working hard. Sometimes they lived hard lives, with a lot of hard work and routine and early mornings, and they gave up a lot. And I think sometimes when they see change, and the rules changing... I wonder if they feel cheated. Or the things that they took on, the rules and regulations or the whole way of life, I think they feel burdened. I just feel sorry for them.

"But for me... have I hope? Have I hope for the Church? I haven't hope for the Church as it is. But that's normal, because it can't survive as it is. Just taking, let's see... in Ireland, the diocesan priesthood. The numbers are dropping, the ones joining the priesthood. You have an aging clergy, and some of the people joining the priesthood are very conservative. It's this big, huge tussle, then, between the conservative and the liberal. It's like you have to fit into one camp. Sometimes I feel you have to walk the middle line. I think Jesus... I always felt that He was a radical, even as a teenager. And sometimes teenagers omit all that, seeing Him as being radi-

54

cal. It's hard to look into the context in which He lived, really, for us. He challenged so much...

"But too much depends on any particular priest in a parish. If he's dynamic and he wants to involve people, then the people will respond. But then he could be moved, and you might get someone who's not interested and wants to keep a tight rein on things. So, I think we're goin' to have to find a different model of Church rather than being clerical or hierarchical. But this is happening in pockets, and I see it in different parishes in the diocese. I've gone into parishes where they have kind of a listening process. Now some priests and religious—some of us—get cynical about this, because you've been at the listening process forever. It's just gathering together different age groups and asking things like, 'What would you like the church to be?' I think you have to move on from that, too, because it can become kind of a griping thing, and priests are always afraid that all their faults are on the block at these meetings ('...he doesn't visit, we don't like his sermons...'). I think we need to get the people who are interested in the Church, because not everyone is, really... 'Cause a lot of Irish people—I don't want to jump the above now; I want to keep the focus on what I'm trying to say—a lot of Irish people go to Mass on Sunday and were taught about religion. It was in our tradition, in our culture. I don't know, I think it's handing over power. It's not just saying, 'Well, I'll make you a reader or a minister of the Eucharist.' That's just a token gesture. I think you really have to just have a sense of being with people, and meet with them, and honestly open up to them. There are so few priests who open up to the people. But it's easy to say that, 'cause it's kind of risky, opening to people. I don't know... is it expecting too much of the priest?

"But I have hope. The young people that I'm meeting through music are interested in singing in church, and they get a buzz when they sing nice stuff and they know, especially at times of mourning, that their singing touches people. They know that. It gives meaning to them. Mightn't be very deep, it might just be that the music was moving to them. But I think that's a lot, because we tie God down too much. Like when I go home sometimes and I walk the fields, and I look around and sometimes I feel that's what's deepest in me. And sometimes it feels like I'm goin' against the grain, with some of the routine that I have to do as a priest, 'cause it's like a job, y'know. One thing I'm not into is regular morning Mass. Having said my Mass for seven years, almost every day and sometimes a few times a day, it kind of grates at you, and I think you lose freshness and it just becomes so boring and mechanical.

"Maybe there's a nostalgia... it's going back to maybe as a child, playing in the fields, being reared there. I find God in nature, in rural Ireland, not the towns. I found it a big change, coming to a town, living in a town... even the noise and the sounds here. When we were at seminary, I got kind of detached from urban life. But living here, it's much noisier than at home. But I find God in nature, in just natural settings. Now, I find Him in the sea, and there's beauty here in this town. But I s'pose for some people, maybe it's just goin' back to where you were born, that sense of your home and your family. That could sound very ideal, because I s'pose more and more of what I'm coming up with, and I s'pose this is coming through what I am saying, is that... putting words around religion and God, I find difficult. When I'm coming to terms with that, and I'm happy with what I'm saying, I think I am experiencing that words are inadequate. And that comes across in my homilies, my sermons, because I get very short with words. And for funerals, I sometimes find using words and all that stuff is kind of arrogant or something, because we've never been there. I think we have to be kind of precious with words. I s'pose in the past, words kinda killed people in sermons. People were denounced, and horrible things were said, angry words, and cruel. So I carefully choose my words. I'm not a spontaneous person in public, in the sermon role, and all that kind of priestly bit…

"So, where God is, is kinda present with me. When I think of Him, I think of maybe the person I thought of as a teenager, that this man, Jesus of Nazareth, was kind of an image. And I would also say in the last few years I've stopped praying for people. I'd be praying for my family, my mother, 'Give me this, give me that.' I've stopped all that. I now say, 'You know all these people, You know their needs.' I think it's kind of growing up about God. He knows all this stuff, like He's not *out there* somewhere. He's here with me, inside me… He's goin' through all this stuff with me, and He knows these people and He knows about them. I know he's not going to work miracles, really, like people with cancer. And I find that's another big part of my life. A lot of people who are dying or sick, and sometimes I just don't want to be there, there at the bedside. I really just want to run away. Sometimes you can get cold about it, 'cause I know when a person is dying, I know they're going to ring up the family, they're gonna come in... I know that horrible pain. And then I'll make the tea. I've been in that situation a lot, and you kind of get used to it. Initially it was hard, but I wouldn't be honest when I say I still feel sadness. I think I haven't learned how to protect myself by not getting too involved emotionally, because I find it very hard, then, getting up the following day, having to give a homily...

"So I have hope because the Church for me is not just a clerical church. I'm looking outside of it. A lot of priests wouldn't see my church as being Church, because they're people who don't go to Mass, and they don't fit in. Some are musicians, and they don't say the Rosary. There are different ways of being 'churched' now. The conservatives would say you must do all this and that... there's a big tussle going on. It's hard to remain true to yourself, because you've politics of the church and you've all of that and the media being drawn in. More and more now, things that you say can be misinterpreted... So I s'pose, maybe it's just as well that I type up my sermons.

"I s'pose we all change, don't we? I'm such a different person from the person I was seven years ago, when I was ordained. I shudder to think what I was like. I was so, well, I was kinda naïve. But I s'pose that's good, because you look back, and you change. I always feel that you can't capture, you know, the way people are at weddings. I'm not into videos, I'm not into photographs, which is interesting, because a lot of people say you should have photographs at holidays and family events. Well, I have some, loads at home, but I feel you can never capture these times. I think you should just go through them, really enjoy them, get the best out of these family days or events, and move on.

"When I was first ordained, I used to go home almost every week... a day off Tuesday or maybe Sunday. Now that I'm into other things, it could be once every three weeks, sometimes once a month, maybe a bit longer. But then I might go home once a week for two or three weeks, or I might not be home for another month."

"Do you have brothers and sisters?"

"I have four brothers—they're married—and I have a sister. I'm closest to my sister. She's younger than me. That often happens. But I think we're getting closer because in the last year she broke up with her boyfriend. It was very hard for her, after seven years. He's working in America. It's a typical Irish scenario. It's like a John B. Keane play… he's the only son, he doesn't want to come back. He would get involved with the farm life and his parents don't kinda get on. So he's kinda over there, staying away from that situation. My sister doesn't want to marry into all that baggage. She's now moved to Cork city. So we meet a lot and we share a lot.

"What are your hopes for the future?"

"I s'pose I'd like to see a Church in the future that was inclusive, that would cope with people's failures and mistakes and the whole spectrum of people in society. And be honest about itself and have less of the politics and the centralization, and the whole control thing. Tony Flannery has kinda mirrored… When I read his book, a lot of that stuff echoed in me, words that he put on things that I would have thought of, but maybe just didn't put the words on. And I think people don't want a perfect Church. It goes back to, the big thing, I s'pose, is the leaders in the Church and priests. Here in Ireland, it's still very clerical. There's goin' to have to be a huge appraisal in the way they're trained. Can they be married? Will they be willing? All of that… Huge ramifications for the Church. I don't know... Am I too hopeful about that in one sense? Married priests and all that? But just a Church that's more open... And that's maybe a very general kind of a phrase, because at the moment in Ireland, I s'pose the leaders are kinda taking cover because they want all this stuff to pass over, and are afraid and all that.

"So, that would be my vision of the future. That's it."

"Thanks, Tim..."

where has it all gone wrong...

Paddy had over thirty years working as a forester, and he knew his country like the back of his hand. After he retired from forestry he became a driver-guide for groups coming to Ireland. The pride and the love he had for his country was so refreshing, clearly reflected in everything he did. Paddy was a natural storyteller, with a keen wit and sense of humor.

"Well, I lived and grew up in the parish of Kildare, underneath the shadow of a famous nun, St. Brigid, probably one of the first nuns in the world, in a sense. St.

63

Brigid is the patron of the dioceses of Kildare and Leighlin, and the patron of the parish of Kildare. On one side of the town, you had the Carmelite Order, known as the White Friars, and then you had the secular priests of the diocese, and then you had the Black Abbey on the other side. So we were probably a little bit more immersed in the religious than would be normal for any other town in Ireland. And I'm not forgetting about the Presentation nuns on one side and the De La Salle Order on the other. So if you grow up in that type of environment and someone asks you to give a dissertation on the religious, you're probably talking to an expert who had to live through, let's say, the entanglements of all those religious orders so congregated in a small town!

"My first introduction to the religious orders was when I was about four, I s'pose. I think I was four. For the pre-school, we were sent to the Presentation nuns, of all things. So as little boys in our short pants, we walked unwillingly to school, I might imagine, because mothers were seen cryin' and wailing, partin' with their beautiful sons. And the sons were bawling like jackasses back out at them. So probably the first day or two the nuns found it more traumatic than we did ourselves...

"We spent a year under their tutelage and uh, waxed,

probably, in strength, wisdom and understanding..."
(Laughter from the listener!) "At the end of the year, we
were deemed to be sufficiently boyish or mature enough
to cross the road into the De La Salle monastery, where
our primary education commenced. In that time, the first
class in the primary would contain sixty fellow criminals! It's the only way to describe it... Some of them
subsequently turned out to be very, very good criminals,
more to a lesser extent. Because at that time, despite a
very good basic primary education, at least seventy to
eighty percent of the people emigrated to England. But
the brothers—the De La Salle brothers—took a great
interest in both the educational and the social and the
sporting aspects. Of course, being from Kildare, we
were involved in football from the time we could almost
walk. Indeed, we had some brothers in Kildare who
spent more time training us to play football than teachin'
us, but that was no harm either, I s'pose...

"Around this time, then, you went from second
class, and you had to learn Irish, math, all the usual subjects. When you got to about ten years of age, if you had
any spark of intelligence, you were asked 'would you
become an altar boy.' And being sort of a rebel, I probably picked the hardest one, because I became an altar

boy for the Carmelites, not in the parish or secular church. And this meant walking a mile and a half in the wintertime for first Mass at 6:30 every morning. Oh, of course, prior to this you had your First Holy Communion. That was a big event. You had to learn your catechism, a little bit of the New Testament, and you had a big exam. Then you went to your first confession and told all your mortal sins at eight or nine years of age, short of murder! You probably hadn't done any mortal sins... In hindsight, definitely no one has mortal sins at that age, but we were fully convinced that we had! And if we didn't have them, the priest didn't know it, but we made them up just to make it sound good. And you got a penance of three Our Fathers, three Hail Marys and somethin' else, maybe. So, you had your First Holy Communion received before you became an altar boy, obviously.

"But the *big* test was when you're in the training class to become an altar boy. Now, this was after school hours. You had to say your responses in Latin. The Mass was in Latin at the time. So you had 'de profundis meas clavias' and stuff like that, all ringin' through your stupid little head! But you learned it, and you were brought then onto the altar and the De La Salle brother went through the motions of the Mass and you had to answer back. You had your gala performance, your first opening night or opening morning at Mass. You weren't allowed to carry the wine or the water for fear you'd spill it with nerves. You weren't allowed to hit the bell, you weren't allowed to carry the patent for the Holy Communion, until you became proficient in all the ways and means of saying and moving the book at the Gospel, and all that...

"I remember once we had an old Carmelite, a Father Walsh. And he was a very funny man. He could say Mass in about fifteen minutes at that. So you really had to be a good altar boy to carry out his attendance, because if you weren't quick enough, he moved the book himself! If you weren't quick enough with the wine and the chalice, he was down in a flash and had that up on the altar and doing the ablutions and the consecrations and everything. The bell he wasn't too worried about... Fifteen minutes was his Mass.

"Until about fourteen years of age we spent serving Mass in the Friary, the White Friary as we called it. In the interim, then, you received your Confirmation, which was another big ordeal. The diocesan examiner, who was appointed by the Bishop, had to ask you two or three questions while you were waitin' anxiously in your new suit to receive Confirmation. So, you went through that, and everything was A-OK.

"When you were fourteen, you had to something called the Primary Certificate. You had to get that in order to go to the secondary school. When you passed that, you moved across to the secondary, and this was gettin' into the serious stuff then. It would still be the De La Salle brothers. You went from first year to second year to third year, and you'd done your Intermediate Certificate. And then you had a final two years to do your Leavin' Certificate, and that probably completed your education at the academic level. The influence of the clergy at this stage had waned.

"But I remember the fast, for example, during those years... You had to be fasting from 12 o'clock the night before. A lot of people were probably cycling and walkin', and in the wintertime it was very harsh weather in the corragh of Kildare. They'd be walking up to five or six miles to Mass, and they weren't even allowed a cup of tea before they'd leave home. And when you think of that for extreme hardship compared to nowadays, you ask, y'know, where has it all gone wrong from the point of view of church attendance and stuff like that...

"In my time in Kildare, I s'pose in lookin' back, they were very enjoyable and laughable days. We had great fun. The brothers were all terribly dedicated men, some dedicated more so to the Gaelic football than teachin', but at least they were dedicated! And those that were dedicated to the teaching were very dedicated. Subsequent to finishin' education and being a lot older, I visited some of them as older men in their seminary in Castletown. And we could have great chats about various little episodes that occurred during our schooling. After that I went on to forestry college and became a forester.

"But in the earlier days, life was a lot more simple and less regimented. The saying of the family Rosary every night was a big event. We couldn't leave the home until the Rosary was said. Mother took a central lead role. At one stage, I remember even apart from all the other prayers and the litany and the 'trimmings' of the Rosary, there was an American priest, Father Peyton— he was the Rosary priest. He drove all the women of Ireland mad! The second year they started saying 'trimmings.' These were prayers, for example, for such things as the conversion of Russia. That was a big prayer meetin' *every* night. And if you were waitin' to go to the pictures, or maybe in later years when you were goin' to the dances, you were tryin' to hurry up Mother. But Mother wouldn't be hurried! We often encouraged the terrier to chase the cat around the kitchen, but Mother would carry on… impervious! Devotion was the central thing of her life, and she wouldn't either look left or right while this was goin' on. She told me years later, when she was quite an old woman, that she knew bloomin' well what was goin' on, and she used to even add extra prayers to further torment us. But we didn't know that at the time…

"Our household was a little bit international. My grandfather was born in the Yukon, in the Gold Rush. His parents died of smallpox in Alaska, and he was sent back as an orphan to Ireland. He was a remarkable man, because he took part in the Great War, and of course his historical accounts of the different battles were first-hand.

"On the other side, then, I had an uncle who was a gambler and whiskey drinker. He was a bachelor, he died a bachelor, eighty-nine years of age. But he led a rather interesting life. Some days his bank account would be completely inflated with his gambling winnins' on the horses, because Kildare was synonymous with horses.

And then, more days of course, it was completely over-drawn. So, he lived a precarious existence. Well, he still lived to be eighty-nine. You'd often wonder... And he smoked and drank whiskey just about every day.

"Every evenin', in the wintertime especially, when the school books were done, we got into some type of debate with my father. It might be over a football match, it might be to do with some item of farm work, but it always wound up in a most heated debate and argument. Almost to such an extent that you'd think there would be someone goin' to be killed. Of course, there was no one ever killed! Because we were all play-acting... Neighbors would come in. We had no television. Radio was the only link you had with the outside world. I remember listening to the famous boxing matches between Sugar Ray Robinson and whoever he was fightin' at the time, and Joe Lewis, and all that era. You depended on the radio for any news or information. We only got the paper once a week.

"All farm operations at that time were communal. One family helped the other, or maybe two or three families together helped one another in the harvesting, the sowing of the crops, the care of the crops. And then, of course, in our county, we had the bogs. The bog was a

71

religion. This is the cutting of the turf. Once you'd have your school holidays, you spent them on the bog, either cutting, wheeling, heaping... And then, of course, the ride home was somethin' spectacular, because you had great races with horses and carts and ponies, all flying along the road. Just like stagecoaches! And of course, we used to watch... every Sunday we had to go to see Roy Rogers, Hopalong Cassidy, the Lone Ranger... all those guys. And of course, with the horses and the carts we used to try to emulate them, and have our own game of cowboys and Indians! You often wonder, life was a lot simpler then, and people probably didn't suffer a lot of the problems of modern-day livin'. We had plenty to eat, of course, but it was of a very basic nature. But people were more healthy, in mind and body, I'd say. So, that's about it that I have to offer on that, for the minute."

"What about the future of the Church? Where do you think it's heading?"

"In Ireland, the Church at the moment is probably at a little bit of a crossroads. That's an understatement. A big crossroads, because younger people have moved away from the Church, and the same degree of devotion and faith is not manifested in the younger population as it would have been in the older population. Sometimes it takes a series of events for people to be brought back into the Church. I'd say the Church has to modernize and maybe clear up its woolly thinkin'. A lot of problems. But still... I'd imagine the Church in Ireland is probably no different from the Church anywhere else in the world. Vocations have fallen off big-time. A lot of the seminaries have closed down. The number of ordinations per diocese now is very small. A lot of parishes have been closed, and big parishes joined with smaller parishes. But I'd imagine that it's more a sign of the times... people have become more materialistic. They're not as conscious even of Christian values as they used to be, apart from being Catholic or Protestant or anything else. People are more materialistic now than, say, being good neighbors... Y'know, on the face of it, the Catholic Church appears to be healthy, but the body of the Church, I think, will have to look differently at the ways of the world. It's taken 'em too long to move with the times, or at least accommodate the new times, the new pressures that people are livin' under.

"This will probably get you into the High Court, or defamation and the whole lot, but my philosophy on reli-

gion is, uh, apart from Catholic, Protestant, whatever…
if people were more Christian in their attitude toward
other people, I think that's of way more importance than
strict religion or the observance of strict religious princi-
ples, which are supposed to help you attain this end. You
don't have to go through all that process to be a good
Christian. You can be a good neighbor, you can believe
in God, you can believe in a Superior Being. Uh, you do
no harm to anyone… As others do to you, do you also to
them in like manner, and all this. That can be all lived
and achieved without religious observance, whether
you're Catholic, Protestant, or whatever. And the phenomenon that exists in most manifest religious observance is that probably the most hypocritical will be the
people who are seen to be present and praying the most.
And this even occurred in another obtuse way in the
Bible, with the people going to the top of the table rather
than being, how do you say it, more humble, and sitting
at the bottom. So I wouldn't see any relationship
between the fall-off in religious observance, and the
ability of a population to live as good Christians,
whether it was Protestant or Catholic, or any other religion. That's the way I look at it." *(Slight pause.)* "Now
you must ask another question…" *(Quiet laughter.)*

"Yes, I could ask lots of questions!"

"Well, ask away! Now is your chance!"

"If you don't go to church..."

"Uh huh...."

"What sustains you, what do you find life-giving?"

"What sustains me is the fact that... Yeah, I see where you're coming from. Me personally might be different than someone else. What sustains me in my attitude to life is... I love working, I love achieving. I have a motivation to do a job well. I delight in seeing the results of my labor, naturally. I like to earn some money. I like to see my wife happy, and my children happy, and my grandchildren happy. The family would be more important to me than anything else. That would be my recipe for a happy life. If you're happy in the happiness you can generate within your family, this is a font of renewal. Whether you can call it spiritual or not, I don't know... And to be happy in your general environment, and happy with the way your immediate life is going, and the direction it's goin'. You have to draw on your own inner strengths to correct any little imbalances that occur in that overall scheme of things. Now, by drawin' on your inner strength, if that inner strength has to be supplemented with religious observance, that might apply to some people, it doesn't apply to me."

"And where do you find God?"

"I find Him *everywhere!* All around me, because... in my job, being a forester and having worked outdoors in nature for almost forty years, you'd have to be very stupid not be aware of the existence of God in the greater scheme of things, in our whole ecosystem. It's all God-created, by a very superior Being, than any one that we can even envisage because, even with our computerization and everything today, I'm doubtful that we could solve the mysteries of the creation of life. It wouldn't be possible. We're able to do wonderful things with medical science, but the actual creation—how the air came into being, how the plants came there, how the hell did we arrive? And all this.... it's, it's such a magnitude that it had to be a superior being, or God, that created all this wonderful environment that we live in. That's where I've been, and draw on that as there being a God. And you also know yourself, when you do something good for someone else… that compunction to do good or to do a good deed. The amount of, how do you say… not pleasure, but well-being that you get from doin' somethin' good. We're supposed to be built in the image and likeness of God. It must be all a part of a chain or a cycle. Of course, the Celts were always great for goin' in circles…" *(He hesitated, watching to see how I responded, and then laughed quietly.)* "Everything in the Celtic psyche is in a circle. We're only part of that circle. The animals are part of it. Every item of Creation. As I said before, you'd have to be very stupid to believe that there wasn't a God. Whether the God is a Catholic God or a Protestant God is immaterial. No one knows…"

"When you say 'Celtic'… Some have mentioned the Celtic Spirit when they've been talking. What do you see as the Celtic origins, what are the roots? The circle is part of it, right… Being close to the earth?"

"Yes… the Celts had such an esteem for all things natural. For example, the Salmon of Wisdom of Finn

77

Mac Cumhail. The Salmon of Wisdom cooking on the fire. He licked his finger and he received all this wisdom. The Celts always related to their animals. The fondness they had for the hunting dog. Finn Mac Cumhail, his two hounds. Everything about Celtic mythology was related to nature... the trees, the storms. Tir na Nog, the man with eternal youth... everything. Also, a story about St. Patrick. ·He came from Rome, but he was clever enough to intertwine all that mythology into our... what turned out to be Catholicism. But it could have been anything. I think the Irish standard of Catholicism wasn't too pleasing to Rome for years and years. Catholicism at this stage in Europe, in European terms, was crazy. You had the Medicis as Popes, you had the Papal Exile in Avignon... three Popes in existence! When you look at the history of Catholicism, it was probably not something to be proud of, to have conducted the Spanish Inquisition in the name of Catholicism, and the destruction of the Inca civilization in the name of Catholicism. We had a whole range of very doubtful strategies. Y'know, doin' away with a culture to supplant it with another one is not always the best thing. We were lucky that Patrick probably had a sense of humor and he realized that we were too stub-

78

born to change, so he inculcated a lot of the Celtic traditions into the religious observances. That's how we came into blessing wells and a whole lot of this and that... as he obviously encouraged the Celts to embrace Catholicism. It goes on today. Every year, we have the blessing of the animals. So the Celts were very close to nature. They had to be. They lived from nature. The very same as your North American Indians. The exact same... They were nomadic, they hunted a lot... fished, farmed. Most farmers are close to nature. The modern farmer has become brainwashed with production, and science, which is not a good thing either. Well, you see the problem is, with population, worldwide now... you have to keep producing."

"What about the way it used to be, the Celtic church, if indeed it could be referred to as a 'church.' Do you think there could ever be a swing or a trend to go back to the roots of Celtic Christianity?"

"No. I'd imagine that our age of monasticism, or even goin' back to the basics, is gone. Because the modern generation, and, conceivably the generations to come, are becoming more materialistic. And that element of the Celtic mystique won't last for very many more generations. Irish people now look more outwardly, to Europe, the different cultures, the Mediterranean. Up until the '60s, the 1960s, we were still basically, even at that stage from the point of view of culture, untouched. We had just barely got television at that stage. A lot of the older traditions even in that thirty-year period, forty-year period, have died out. Someone was asking me about trick-or-treat on Halloween, and all this dressing up for Halloween, and St. Stephen's Day. All those old traditions are dead. When we moved here thirty years ago, on St. Stephen's Day kids would come here singin' at the door and you'd have money ready for 'em, pennies. I think the last few Christmases we had no one, absolutely no one, who came. These were all based on Celtic traditions. They're all gone..." *(Pause.)* "Just progress! Progress..." *(Another pause.)* "Y'see, even educationally now. A lot was lost from the mystique by changing the liturgy into English, in the church. That's getting back to your question about revertin' to the Celtic. Latin has always played a big part, right back to Caesar's Gaelic War, in say, the religion of the sixth, seventh, eighth centuries, when Ireland was the island of saints and scholars. All the liturgy was Latin—Vespers and Matins and all that. That changeover, probably from my generation, had a big impact. We said the Mass wasn't the same. Who knows? Probably a lot of people were lost by that changeover. That was as a result of Vatican II. But it mightn't have been the best... Y'see, the Irish church probably was nationalistic in a sense as well, whether we like it or not; it had suffered a lot under the penal laws, and right up until 1916, so much was under suspicion by the British, especially. It was closely identified with the people. A lot of the people who were attendin' Mass didn't know in the name of hell what had happened. Yet they were very prayerful, though. There was this system in Ireland where the Latin Mass was goin' on, but you'd see the old guy and the old lady with the Rosary beads sayin' the Rosary. That had no relationship to the Sacrifice of the Mass.

"I don't know how you could say that we'd ever revert to being really Celtic in even our outlook now, because our outlook now is very cosmopolitan. The Celts probably lived very much within their own community. That's not at all possible. I don't think there's any place on earth now that's not influenced by outside events." *(Slight pause.)* "Any more questions?"

(Smiling.)

81

"Is there anything you'd want to say to your grand-children as they grow up?"

"Oh, I'd like to see them living a good life, working hard, rearing their families, doing the best they can. I wouldn't try to dictate what any generation would do. I think every generation has to find its own level. I think it's the way it always was, but as you get older, you're not inclined to think so. Every generation has its own problems. In the '20s, 'twas this bloomin' can-can dance—not the can-can dance, the...."

"The Charleston?"

"The Charleston. Exactly. This was completely out of bounds. You know, every generation had all these things. So, ten to one, we'll come back to being 'good' folk again at some stage, but we mightn't be Celtic! I'm only jokin'...

"Probably the biggest problem in the world is drugs. I'd more afraid of drugs than anything else. I think kid-s'll be kids. They're goin' to make mistakes. You're not goin' to stop 'em. A lot of the innocence of the young has been lost. It's probably to do with television. It has to do with a lot of things..." *(A rather wistful smile.)* "In our day, growin' up, we were very—how would you say? Naïve and innocent. But you don't get that anymore now. It's a sign of the times. I dunno, I see young people, I'm dealin' with 'em every day, and I admire 'em. They're very assertive, and they work hard. I admire 'em... because it is a tough world, highly competitive. When I was growin' up, it wasn't. Y'know, if you done well, you done well, and if you didn't do well, you didn't do well, and no one would worry about it. Nowadays, everybody will get uptight if they have a guy who's not performing well. That puts pressure on 'em."

"Thank you... thank you so much, Paddy."

SOMETIMES A STAR...

he would be
my main man...

Miriam was one of the younger generation, eager to share some of her thoughts and feelings. Once again, she was very articulate, like so many I spoke with, and seemed comfortable as well. Her birthday was the following day. She would be twenty-one.

"I s'pose a lot of people my age would be in third-level education—college.

They would be in college, and working part-time jobs. Most people would be in different courses, like in law, or counseling. I'm doing counseling, introduction to

85

counseling, in college. Most everyone my age, with luck, would be balancing the two—college and work—which is very hard. So you're out on your own, on your own two feet, y'know, tastin' a little of reality. Like, afterward, you would move out of your home and gain your own independence and try to make a livin' and build for the future. I s'pose there's a lot of emphasis on education for me at the moment, furthering my education and learning. That would be my goal anyway, to achieve. I'm off doin' two courses in college. Last year I did a medical/dental secretarial course, so this year I then went on. I wanted to go deeper, really... I wasn't sure if I was going to do medical or counseling. So next year I'll hopefully be going into UCC [*University College Cork*] and then take a psychology course in early childhood studies. And most people my age have the same idea, maybe they're in law or they're in business, building up step-stones, maybe to have a comfortable life, a good job. A lot of people maybe think of money, the money side. But for me, I think, the reason I do it myself—go to college and further my education—would be to have a job that I'd have an interest in, something I would look forward to goin' to in the morning. The money comes fairly down the line on the list for me. But I obviously would think of the money to buy a house and have a family... down the line.

"The social scene now for my age group would be a lot different over here. I was away in Germany last week for the week, and it's so different. It is really different, the social scene. I find over here... like friends meet up and go out to the pub, and they can just drink and drink, almost like, you don't remember it anymore, remember the night out or that you're so sick. That's it. Everyone just gathers in groups and meets in pubs, and then goes to clubs afterwards. It's, it's the abuse of alcohol, maybe, here it would be higher. Not like, they wouldn't be alcoholics, but the social scene, it's so different than it would be in Germany. It's empty answers and drink and maybe getting drunk. It's what we call 'craic', or havin' a laugh.

"Over here, you go into a pub just to drink. To get something to eat is just peanuts, maybe. But over in Germany it would be more of a restaurant and a pub, all in one, like a bistro rather than just a pub. You can purchase a meal. In Germany, you go in and people are ordering beer, and maybe after two beers, people started ordering food and meals and they'd bring out trays of food. They'd maybe get a bottle of wine with the meal, and just slow the pace down. Everyone really enjoyin' themselves and socializin', but not getting drunk, and not this attitude of 'we have to get drunk or we're not goin' to have a good night...' Life is different, and the atmosphere in the pubs, like background music, is more relaxing. The emphasis is more on talking to people, and being able to talk. But the pubs in Ireland, it's like you're hoarse from having to shout over the roar. Here it's just loud music and drink. So there's a big difference, which I find hard now goin' out at night, just goin' into a pub. If you could have a mixture... Like, if you want to go for something to eat here, you have to go to a restaurant. If you want something to drink, then you have to go to a pub. So, like, if they could mix the two maybe more... Like if you were maybe in kind of a restaurant, like in Germany, where maybe you could get beer and you could get food, maybe alcohol wouldn't be abused as much by the social scene, maybe it would be altered a little. But my age group, definitely, on Saturday night in the city center there are so many people drunk and people falling down. So many young people my age falling around and not remembering anything. Maybe it's not just for my age group, but I notice it maybe a little bit more. People seem to go to college for the whole week and maybe work at part-time jobs, only to live for the

Saturday night out in the pub, goin' out around 7 o'clock, just drinkin' for the night, and then goin' clubbing. When the pubs close, they go to the clubs..."

"What's the difference between going to the pubs, and then 'clubbing'?"

"A club, it's practically the same, except it's open from about 11 o'clock. It would be just loud music, and getting more drink. And it has a dance floor. In a pub you don't have a dance floor, you just have little tables and counters. In the club you'd have counters, side counters, where you put your drink on, and you're just dancin'. And they close at 2:30.   There are different clubs with different types of music, a lot o' times really loud. You'd have dance music, you'd have maybe chart music, pop music... A mixture, really. And we have a lot of clubs in our city for college students, where it would be a cheaper rate to get in. The age limit would be maybe eighteen. In a lot of other clubs, it could be twenty-one... they're aged off like at twenty-one, twenty-three, twenty-five. Twenty-five would be the oldest, and obviously people our age then wouldn't get into these, they would be for the older people. There would be a little under-age drinking as well. A lot of young people get into these clubs... girls sixteen, seventeen, can dress up and wear lots of make-up and little skirts and little tops. They don't know if they're older, so... We have to show IDs... sometimes, but not all the time. If you're a student, you have a student card and you just present it at the door to the bouncers, and they want to see your date of birth."

"Are these primarily on Saturday nights?"

"Yeah. Well, during the week, like on a Monday night is a college night. It's cheaper than, say, a normal night in town. For a pint of beer it would be like two-fifty. And, say, a Tuesday night it would be cheaper, which encourages maybe, strengthening more... the drinking. Then they'd have different venues, like on a Tuesday night it could be a lot less to get into a club, and like on a Saturday night it would be more. So it kind of encourages the social scene, maybe, for young people during the week. The prices would be more expensive heading towards the weekend. Mondays, Tuesdays, Wednesday nights, then, would be mostly young people eighteen to twenty-five out socializing. The social scene would be geared for young people, generally.

"You mentioned earlier that the social scene is not as important, for you, still."

"For me, no, not as important. I don't have this emphasis on havin' to get drunk to have fun. I can make a balance. Like, I love going out and meeting—it's good to meet with friends and go to a pub, but to be aware that I don't have to abuse alcohol and that I can sit there and have one or two beers and still have a good night, meet all my friends and have a chat and just a little bit of cra-ic."

"Would they have the same idea? They don't get drunk either, your friends?"

"Some would have that idea, having a good chat, and having fun with your friends, and maybe going to a club afterwards and dancin'. So I'd say I'm one of the lucky ones that haven't got the idea in my head that I have to drink and maybe do drugs. So I am lucky in that. Now, that's my attitude, a little bit more mature, maybe. Some of my friends, there'd be one or two, that definitely don't drink. It's really fun to go out with these people because they don't drink, they don't do drugs. You can

91

have so much fun! When I've been out socializing with this particular group of friends, then I find that I don't drink either, 'cause they're not drinking. So it does rub off on me. And I don't even need to drink. I won't even have a pint of beer. I'll have a Coke, and be out dancin'. It's the same. The difference is that you have more money!" *(A little laugh!)* "It's amazing, you come home from a club and you spent far less than if you had been drinking. When I don't drink, I still have so much fun, and you can remember it. You wake up in the morning and are fresh and not sick, you don't have a hangover. You remember the night, everything that happened. There are no black places, it's like a hole there, and I think that's really good..."

"Now, tell me... what about Church? Have you stopped going? And could you tell me why?"

"I actually don't believe in the Church, but I have belief in God, and that there is something more powerful than all of us humans. I thoroughly have a strong belief in that... and I do pray. When I pray, I make it very personalized, to my level. I don't feel like maybe I'm lookin' up, high up to something that's so powerful that I'm afraid of it..." *(She put her hands together in a praying gesture and looked up toward the sky.)* "I feel like there is a God, and He's a higher power than me, but... I kinda make a picture in my head of someone not frightening, maybe very powerful, but someone human. Maybe in jeans and a jumper [*sweater*] that I can have the same level to, and that I don't feel like it's overpowering me. And I get a very strong feeling when I talk. I have a saint that I talk to, St. Martin, St. Martin de Porres. I find him very interesting. I feel a kind of pull towards him. He would be my main man. I do believe in God and Mary. I often feel like they are a higher power, of very strong influence, but I can maybe be a little apprehensive in going to them or really talking and praying to them..."

"The big guys!"

"The big guys! So, St. Martin is really like myself. He lived a very normal type of life, just like me in a way, so I can relate to him, rather than tryin' to understand like the Immaculate Conception and all that, which I do really have very strong feelings about, but it's something you can't really explain. Or maybe I don't bother myself

93

trying to work it out. I believe in it... I mean, I do have strong belief in the Holy Spirit and the Trinity, so I do believe and I do pray, like to Mary and to all different saints.

"There's a chapel in the city center devoted to St. Martin de Porres, and I often will just go in there and just sit in the chapel. Now, I don't have a structure of prayer. I just sit there and generally talk to him, like, 'St. Martin, it's like this... this isn't working,' or 'St. Martin, be with me today,' and he'll definitely be with me in the situation and I'll thank him and show appreciation. But where Mass is concerned, I don't feel the closeness when I go into Mass. In fact, in Mass, I don't feel close to any of what I believe in. I can't say that it's boring, because it *is* meaningful. But it's too structured, it's too formatted. Like you go to Mass, everyone is sitting there, listening to the priest. Dad says I have to receive the Eucharist to really believe. That's not my idea! If I was going up to Mass every Sunday and receiving the Eucharist, and living my life with no God in it... I think that would be a lot worse. I think that would be a bit hypocritical, really. Or goin' to Mass, and receivin' the Eucharist, or goin' to Confession, and I don't believe in anything and I don't pray. So I have more meaning from my own God, and I talk to Him all the time... but I don't go to Mass. Sometimes the priests will make me feel guilty because, all my life Mom and Dad would take us to Mass and they taught us about religion, and in school they always talked about religion, and maybe this was the thing we were taught to do, that goin' to Mass every Sunday is Christianity. But when I grew up, I developed my own ideas. I think that my own ideas are good as well, and that I have belief, and that I do pray. I have meaning enough, like I get a sense, a feeling, that when I am talking or praying to whoever it may be, I have a feeling over me of closeness. It's good. And I don't get it in Mass. I really don't... Maybe that's sad, but I don't. I just don't..."

"You're not alone. I think a lot of people, especially young people, are feeling that way."

"But then, if ever I have children, then I would do what my mom and dad did, teach them about religion and maybe the way that it's structured. Like, the Bible is very interesting... there's so much reading in that. And I would be interested in that. I would teach them the Bible and I would bring them to Mass, to the stage that they

95

would be able to find out, could find a God, their own God, that they understand, and take the meaning of that for themselves. Rather than say, 'You have to go to Mass until you're eighteen,' and maybe drive them away. I would want them to understand the Mass, and every part of the Mass, and know the prayers in the Mass. That would be very important to me, that they would know that, and at whatever age they could develop their own ideas, they could choose whether they wanted to keep goin' to Mass and receivin' the Eucharist." *(Pause.)*

"I s'pose, at the moment I think a lot about life after death. Heaven and earth, really. I feel really strongly that maybe this is heaven and this is earth, and it's altogether contained. That this is heaven here, and this is earth, and it's all combined into one. And maybe when we die, we die, and maybe that's it. Like, when I was a child, I always thought, are we goin' to be going to heaven? And my view of heaven was the clouds. Flying out to Germany last week, the day I was flying, I was in the clouds. And I felt, y'know, this was heaven. I always pictured, like with my nan... she's dead now. I used to picture her in heaven, heaven would be in the clouds. And even being in the sky the other day, and thinking, no... this isn't heaven. It looks like heaven. And to look out at the fluffy clouds, and just feel like you could maybe dance from one to the other. And I said to myself, this is a picture of heaven, maybe, that I'd like it to be. Something peaceful and tranquil, and pretty to look at. I hold onto that. Maybe somehow they are here, my grandparents, and that I can't see 'em physically. That confuses me a little.

"Y'know, there are so many people on this earth. There are so many bad people, yet there are so many good people, just generally good people, really. They treat others well, with respect. Like with your friends, they would have respect and caring for each other, and I think in a way, that is heaven. To be able to have relationships with other people, and friendships that are pure and sincere, and in a way that's a taste of heaven. But then, there come the evil, nasty people, and that's a taste of hell, d'ya know what I mean? And we're experiencin' it all, on this earth…"

"And, does anyone have the answers? We can choose, really… We can choose whether we think that nothing happens after death, or believe 'yes, there is something'…"

"We can! Because no one can tell us whether it's right or wrong. But I like to believe that, when I think of my grandparents. When my grandmother died and was buried, and it was reassuring to me, that my grandfather was there, wherever, and they're reunited. I do feel that. And I feel that someday, like all the family, when we all eventually do die out, we will be reunited. And we'll be meeting people—relations, maybe, that we never met! I do believe in that. And I choose to believe in that, and I get a nice feeling from it. Something like, there's hope. Yeah, definitely. And I do say that my grandparents are together, they're reunited again. I like to think that, after so many years... maybe twenty years, maybe longer, because Mom was just married. So, like after all those years, they'd be reunited. That is a really fulfilling thought.

"But I do believe as well that on the day we're born, we have a path that is made out to us, and that we just fall into it, and everything is like a hidden plan for us. We can alter it maybe, just a small bit, by different decisions we make in our lives, but that definitely, we have one kind of a road and that we will follow it. We have no choice. But I like the feeling to be aware of it, d'ya know? I like looking into things. Well, I like studying psychology, like analyzing things. And when I look in and see, like this time last year, what I was doing... and now the changes in my life. The connections, the little bridges... and to look back, and think, 'Right, I won't be here this time next year.' You couldn't possibly be! Just to look at the little connections, there's something stronger here than just me, that there's some power here, that is creating this jigsaw puzzle, and as you go along, the little pieces just fill in. I look at it as a positive thing. It's interesting, that I have a plan... and to find what it is. And I wouldn't be stressed. I like to believe that there's something here for me, that I am worth something as an individual and that I have been given a task. Maybe I don't know yet, but, someday I will. Y'know, well, it's a constant journey, from the time you are born right up to when we die. At the moment, I s'pose my age, like being twenty, twenty-one, I'm very aware of all this. I think it's my age. And that to me it is my religion, and it is my belief as well... very strong. Because if I didn't believe, I wouldn't have this jigsaw and couldn't make these connections. It is all definitely a higher power... and that's good.

"So, if people say to me, 'You don't go to Mass,' I get aggravated. What's the point of me goin' to Mass when I don't feel anything, when my belief is so strong and my own ideas are so strong. I do believe in something. I don't try to explain it... it can't be explained. I think it's a lot healthier than maybe goin' to Mass and not having any interest in Communion—everything. I have a lot of candles for St. Martin de Porres, and pictures of Our Lady. In fact, I have a medal of Our Lady— it is very special. It's from Lourdes. There's a picture of the shrine at the back of it, in Lourdes. I just don't look at it as fashionable, but it has very strong meaning to me. D'ya understand? I do believe that this could keep me safe in my everyday journey through life. And when I was flying... I was a bit nervous at flying, and at take-off. And I would think maybe somethin' might happen. So I just gave the medal a little kiss. That's my belief. And if I'm goin' through a very hard time, I sit down just to have a little chat, just talk it out, very normally, like I was just talkin' to maybe my mom or someone very human. It's not someone bending down to me, and feeling 'you're too powerful for me ever talk to you, so I have to word this right.' I can say it straight out, what I'm thinking. And afterward I get this feeling that, say, maybe the little black hole that I had is being filled or brightened or opened up, like a flower. I s'pose that's my

100

experience. It's hard to explain it. I get a warm feeling, maybe... and it's then I can come back. I always feel better."

I asked if she ever talked with anyone about these feelings, and she said yes, her mother.

"She understands. It would be harder to talk to Dad because, um, he's very strong in his belief. I s'pose just like I would be as well. Dad would often say, 'Oh, you never go to Mass,' and I would just say, 'Yeah, but I do believe. And I have my belief.' Maybe once or twice we'd have a little argument, and I'd say, 'But I believe, and I pray to St. Martin de Porres.' Dad just couldn't go along with it. 'No, you have to receive the Eucharist.' But Mom understands. I often have these conversations with Mom and talk to her a lot. Mom will give me maybe little prayers. Like, Mom brought this back from Lourdes. Y'know, little things like that.... Even though the way Mom and Dad brought me up maybe to go to Mass every week, Mom totally accepts my belief. And it's really good that she understands and that I can talk to her. With Mass and everything, her reaction would be maybe that I should receive the Eucharist, but I do think

101

that, well, what I'm doing at the moment and my attitude towards my religion, I believe she thinks is good. Because it is, it is… I tell her what I feel sometimes. And maybe it's the same that she gets that feeling in Mass, what I get in my own prayer. Maybe we can relate that we do it, which is interesting. And Mom gives me a lot of books as well, to read on my own. D'ya know Anthony De Mello?"

"Oh, yes!"

"So I'm doing a lot of reading. Those sort of books on spirituality. And I really enjoy them. So they give me a balance, and maybe I prefer to do it this way rather than go to Mass. It must be very sad, y'know, not to have belief or not to have a feelin' of a higher power, y'know. A person would be very empty without that feeling, maybe…"

"What book are you reading of Anthony De Mello?"

"I'm reading 'Awareness' and I've read 'The Heart of the Enlightened'. When I started this course in September—Introduction to Counseling—a lot of it was personal development, which was very interesting."

"It's a fascinating field, especially if you like people. You may have a future in doing some counseling—because so much of it is talking with people, and listening, and being encouraging..."

"And being understanding, and being there for people, d'ya know? Especially people that feel their life has been empty, or a bit lost, maybe. You can encourage them, and let them know you can comfort them."

"Comfort them, and also help to show them that they have choices. There are certain skills that you get to learn after a while, to show how empowering it is to know that people have choices. We can choose to really go on a downward spiral, or we can choose to make something of our lives..."

"It's all in the choice..." *(Smiling)*

"Very empowering."

"Yeah. I work it out myself sometimes. I say to

103

myself, 'You have to do this... ' 'don't put it so strong' You have to do it, but you don't. But if you don't, it will be very costly. Well, then, I choose to do it because it'll make things easier, or whatever. And you'll have a good feeling, maybe, afterwards."

"Are you taking classes at night?"

"No, it's during the day. Three days. We're doin' psychology, we're doin' sociology, and personal development."

"And you're working part-time as well! What are you doing?"

"Retail. It's not great. But I have a balance. I do something for Monday, Tuesday, and Wednesday that I really enjoy and get a lot from. And Thursday, Friday, Saturday, it's like my mind goes to sleep, or just not working. It's not interesting, you just go about... You have to go. You have to make money. And then the other side is so in-depth and, y'know, interesting. It's a balance. And that's good! A variety..."

"Ideally, if you can find what you love to do is also what you can earn a living in. For a lot of people, it's one or the other. Like for instance, their hobby might be photography or music. But what they really love, they can't seem to be able to do as a livelihood."

"And maybe that's what I hope for. I hope for that... to go into some field like psychology, or in that line, that I will be able to balance, that I really enjoy it, and I'll be interested in it. That would be my number-one priority. And then to be able to make money, to live comfortably..."

"That idea of being on a path is wonderful. And then, can you also look back on your life and see where you got off? Being aware that God, or a higher power, has a path for each of us...Often we can look back over the years and see, 'Oh, I wasn't on my path. But I am now!' And see where we sometimes even go off a little bit, and then we have to make some adjustments to get back on."

"We're diverted, yeah. Well, that's, I s'pose, where the choices are. We're kinda always making choices that will bring us back, right? To me, anyway; I think to myself if I'm feeling fallen off the path a bit, and then I ask Him to help me to get back on. And He does…"

"And that He's always there, and He forgives. Very quick to forgive. He's not a judging God that a lot of us were brought up with… as being a rather severe God, a punishing God."

"And to be afraid of… That's not my God."

"No. And it isn't my God either! My God is a loving God, and a forgiving God… and just wants us to come back…"

"…with open arms!"

"Right!"

"That picture…"

"Beautiful."

"And it's not something that's goin' to condemn

106

us... I remember for a long time I felt very angry at God, maybe when I was younger, when my grandmother died. I was around fifteen. I was into religion and doubt, trying to understand. I was just at that age and was questioning, and inquisitive. I remember I was with my sister and I said, 'If there is a God there and He's so great, how can He make everybody feel so sad?' D'ya know what I mean? To take Nan away and to have us be so sad and feel so awful... 'There can't be a God.' In school, in religion class, I used to be so disruptive, I said, 'There is no God!' I had a lot of anger at Him. But I think He really stayed with me even more!"

"You wouldn't be alone there! There are lots of stories of when the saints were angry with God! So, you would certainly not be alone. Just the fact that you do talk to God, or talk to St. Martin or some of the saints, is all you really need... comfortably so, relaxed..."

"But it's so natural... instead of saying 'O most Gracious God' and being so rigid. There's a poem, 'Footprints.' Do you know it?"

"Yes."

107

"It's amazing. I really love that. When I feel maybe a bit down, I always read that. I know it so well. When it comes to the end part and says, 'Lord, when I really needed you, there was only one set of footprints…' I know the times when he was carrying me."

"This was wonderful! Thanks so much, Miriam."

"Thanks for talking with me. It was interesting for me as well to be able to give my own opinions."

out of the frying pan, into the fire...

A Conversation with Tony Flannery

We began our dialogue with a reference to one of Fr. Flannery's books, 'From the Inside.' In it he mentioned that he had found there was a different, what... spirit in the church, particularly in parts of Sligo and Athenry. They were utilizing more of their gifts, like mime, and theatre, and music in the liturgy. I asked him if he had any afterthoughts once the book was in print.

"Not particularly now, Margo, because that book was really just a particular stage. And like it's not the end of my life. I would hope to write more... So in that sense, I don't see that as a final statement on anything. I see it very much as a statement of where I was at when I wrote that book. Already I would write a different book. It's several years now since I wrote that one, and if I was writing one now, it would be different. 'Cause things are moving on so fast, and I'm moving on so fast! Just by coincidence, you mentioned Sligo, which was a case where I saw some real signs of life in something I was doing there two years ago. I'm due to be part of a team going down next month to the Cathedral parish, to do a big Novena. And just the other day, the man in charge of the monastery where I live got word that I was not welcome there anymore. The bishop does not want me. Another side of Sligo, and it's another side of the Irish Church... and that's not surprising. You have, on the one hand, big efforts to do things, yet... Sligo is a smallish town, around two thousand. The cathedral is St Anne's, and it was St Anne's I was in—we were doing a week's retreat, a mission. There were some great priests there, and the place was really buzzing now, y'know, and there was this excellent group of lay people who so much wanted to be involved and were so creative and so talented... and so committed! Marvelous to see...

"The Cathedral is ruled over by a very conservative bishop who is at the other end of the spectrum. He wants us to go there and do very traditional things. He wants us to go into the confession box, while these are people who have to go in and make their confession to us in the box. He doesn't even believe in the Celebration of Reconciliation. But that's very typical of the Irish church at the moment. You have aspects that are representative of the Church of the 1940s, side by side with a real struggling to bring a new Church into birth. And where is it going to go and which is going to be dominant, that's the big question. When I'm in a bad mood and depressed, I would say the old will have its way...

"Same in Cobh... that group that I met around Tim Fouhy. They were impressive. They were mostly involved in the Taize Mass and they were involved in the choir. But they were alive, and they were enthusiastic about the Church and religion! And to meet that now in Ireland today is so refreshing. On the other hand, you have the official church around the bishop there, which is solemn and stately and oppressive in so many ways. And there they are, side by side on one little island. Very interesting..."

Laughing, Fr. Flannery then said, "I'm smiling! Ask some more questions!"

"When we were talking earlier, I mentioned that there seems to be a lot of anger and a lot of pain in both the young people and the middle-aged. You said yes, and there's sadness... Could you say a little more about that?"

"I will. In a minute now... I wonder about the anger in the young generation. In a way, they have no reason to be angry. Our generation has much more reason to be angry than they have."

"One young man, while we were sitting up on a hill overlooking the cathedral, seemed to direct his anger at the building. He said, 'Look at that monstrosity. Look at those spires. They're like spikes.'"

"What do you think of that cathedral? The building?"

"I think it's beautiful!"

112

"I thought so too..."

"And when it's lit up at night, it's just... It's like a vision. And yet the irony of it is... that there's so much anger and pain directed toward the Church and certain clergy that have been, well, let's say abusive, from some of the stories they've related. And yet the Church remains... in its glory! Such a paradox, and a contradiction."

"You're right there. You're right there... yes. And Cobh, if I were asked to pick a spot in Ireland that was more prevalent in the traditional life of Catholicism, it would be Cobh. Which is interesting, because there you land. The first time I worked there, I think it was in 1980, the big thing that struck me was the extraordinary size of the church. Even the location of the buildings and the cathedral. Did you see the six priests' houses behind it? And the bishop's house in back? They really dominate the town, y'know, and even in terms of property and that. It was more clerically done. It is by far the most clerical church I have ever experienced, the church in Cobh, in the early '80s. And some of my confreres in the Redemptorists could go back farther and tell stories of even more clerical times.

"We were visiting the people. Ireland in the 1980s was an economically bad time. There was massive unemployment, and Cobh was hit more than most because the steel works had just closed down, and the Dunlop factory in Cork and the Ford factory in Cork. So, that whole area had been hit in the late '70s, early '80s, by massive unemployment. Now, it has improved a lot since then. But when we were visiting the estates, places like that, they were very angry. They were angry over the power, dominance, and seeming wealth of the Church. One of the things to just focus on... y'know, the six houses at the back of the cathedral? There is a car park between the cathedral and the six houses where the priests park their cars. Strange phenomenon about priests in Ireland. They are actually not well off, and they are not well paid. But they do tend to spend whatever money they have on their cars! If you were ever at a conference of priests, the cars outside would be almost completely new cars. And you know in Ireland, y'see, you can see that just straight away because you know the way we register our cars today? The year is on them... So, go to a conference of priests and they'll be all new cars. The sight of the six good cars outside the priests

114

big houses just drive the people of Cobh mad. 'There they are, living in their luxury, telling us how to live. And they know nothing about life.' That sort of thing. There was an awful lot of that. And at that stage the fall-out was really beginning. In the estates, people have stopped going to Mass. Now I think in Cobh, Mass is down twenty-five percent, thirty percent, something like that. But, y'see, the young generation, the twenty-year-olds, wouldn't have experienced the oppression of the Church, like, say, we would have experienced it. But anyway, that's besides the point... sadness..." *(Very audible sigh, long and drawn out.)*

"I'm living in a monastery of twenty-eight people, and there are four or five of us who are not getting the pension. So, twenty-two or -three out of the twenty-eight are getting the pension. It's the biggest income in our monastery. In other words, what I'm sayin' is that I'm living in a home... it's like bein' in an old people's home. Our season tends to go from, our work season, from September to June, and July and August are quiet months with us. So that the beginning of September we have meetings and we have planning and all that sort of thing, getting back into work. But it's just pathetic, sitting around with this group of old men, most of whom

115

are retired. A lot of 'em are invalids, and a few of whom are still trying to struggle on, going out preaching some. I am the second youngest in the house, and I'm in my fifties. It's very hard to cling to any sort of youth when you're living in a situation like that. I mean, when I joined that community over thirty-five years ago, I didn't bank on that. I joined something that would give me life, and now I'm there, and it's not giving me life anymore. And it's not just me! It's not giving life to the one young fellow in the house who's twenty-eight. I had a long chat with him this morning. I've developed the coping mechanisms, and he hasn't. It's dreadful for him, and I'm trying to say to him, 'Go... go, go anywhere... just go! If you stay here long you'll be dead.' So, that would be a big aspect of the sadness.

"As you know, I'm not a great admirer of the Irish Church of the past. I think there was an awful lot that was dreadful about it. But there was also an awful lot that was great about it. The notion of service was so strong. 'Live your life for others, not for yourself'—that was so strong. And that's a beautiful thing. The young generation now is being taught only opposite messages. I think that's very sad, and I think it's sad that so much of what was so beautiful about it has been swamped by

116

what was bad about it. Now maybe in time, I'm sure in time, it will get back into perspective again. But right now 'tis all the badness and all the oppression and all the injustice and all the ugliness of the traditional Church. And that's sad... Things like that.

"Last night, I was talking to another one of our men, talking with him on the phone. He's in a mess. He joined in his mid-twenties, so he's been thirteen, fourteen years with us now. He's been ordained for about ten. He is brilliant. He's one of the best preachers I know. I've worked a lot with him, and boy, he's great to work with. But now he's alcoholic, he's had a nervous breakdown, and his life is falling apart. The community he's living in, which is very similar to mine... there's nothing there to sustain him. And that's very sad. I said to him, 'Go and find a life somewhere else.' And I hate that! Damn it, I didn't join religious life for that! But that's where we've come to... All of that sort of thing, now, Margo... the collapse of something that was once so rich..."

"In the midst of all that, what does sustain you?"

"That's assuming I'm being sustained." *(A wry sort of laugh.)* "Oh, it's a big struggle at the moment.

117

Undoubtedly, it's a struggle. I still love the work. I love the ministry. I still very often believe... Well, I believe it a lot less, I was thinking about it just then. So many goin' around preachin', do they actually believe anymore? But the core message of Christianity would mean much more to me now than ever before, the sort of fundamental message. And the sense that you can actually bring some sort of feeling into people's lives, by presenting the Christian message in its purity and its purest strength..."

"Which is...?"

"Which is... Oh, it has to do with, uh..." *(Long pause.)* "You see, we're straight away now onto what is a big problem, which is finding language. And that is massive in Ireland, trying to find language in which to express this reality that won't sound like a cliché or sound old or stale. That's a big problem for preachers."

"It's a struggle, but I think it has to be done. All of us, not just Ireland. Everywhere."

"Oh, absolutely... of course, of course... But by and

large, we're failing to do that in the Irish Church. And I think that is part of the reason why we've lost the young people. In a way, it's a problem of belief, it's a problem of the institution, but it's also massively a problem of language. For me, the big thing would be the notion of freedom, the notion that the Christian faith leads to the fullness of life and a freedom to live. To live that life, that is, that you won't find anywhere else. Now, when you're trying to preach that in the Irish context, you're preaching it very often to people who experienced the Christian faith as exactly the opposite of that. They've experienced it as narrow and oppressed and restrictive. And that makes it difficult. But it also makes it very hopeful, because there is a great sense of upsetting people's faith, and saying, 'For God's sake, y'know, the things that you've worried all your life about, the things that you feel guilty about, the things you've been a failure in. They're really not important things at all.' And trying to get people to focus on the reality of God and God's message, and God's Presence and God's love for them... That would be the focus, rather than to focus on themselves and their own symptoms, and their own failure and their own feelings of guilt." *(Another sigh.)* "I feel there's an awful lot there that's good to do, and I can

119

do it reasonably well. So that sustains me, and that gives me energy. Monastic life doesn't anymore. I barely lived it. I'm out of it more than in it. I hook up to friends in my life who are very important to me, and I tend to live my life around them rather than around my monastic community. Now, *that* is not the way to live, traditionally, either. But I guess I want to say that the reality of the religious life is here" *(gesturing with his hand to his heart).* "That is the only way I can sustain it..."

"At the end of the book ('From the Inside'), and you just said that a few minutes ago... You mentioned the Church as being oppressive and controlling. In the last few pages, you said you would like to see the Church enabling us to be mystics. If I remember correctly, the question you asked was, 'Are bishops mystics?'"

"How many of the people attending the Council are mystics. I s'pose the contrast there, you see, is between the church person as a functionary and almost as a civil servant. You know what I mean by that? What civil servants are? There's the American equivalent of that... The civil servants are the people who run the institutions of government. They sit in the offices and make decisions, that sort of thing. So much of what goes on in the Church is driven by that sort of institutional thing that would have to keep the system going, and that involves this, this and this. Yet at the other level, so much of the Church that we tend to know, as young people growing up in the '50s and '60s, was very much a church of laws. Somebody talked about that just this morning: why is salvation always such a big factor in Christianity? So, if you do this, this, this and this, you will be saved. If you don't, you won't. There was so much of that about it. I'll do what I'm told, I'll be safe, and I'll be a good faithful member of the institution..." *(Pause.)* "The notion of the mystic... hmmm."

"Seeing God everywhere... seeing the Divine?"

"The Divine, yeah, maybe more than God now. Because I think the notion of mystic... it's important to keep it in as broad a context as we possibly can. So the sense that there is more to life than what appears on the surface, and to have that sense about all aspects of life. To be in touch with the Mysteries—language is a big problem here, of course—but that sense of being in touch with Mystery, and being open to Mystery...

121

"I see a big contrast in those two attitudes to religion, 'cause the person who is down the line keeping the Commandments, saving his soul, cannot possibly have moved to this, this sense of wonder, which would lead you into Mystery. You're too contained, you're too corralled... tied in. So you need to be set free from that before you can become a mystic. Y'know, obviously, in the Catholic tradition, 'mystic' is John of the Cross, Teresa of Avila. We have used that word very narrowly. I'm trying to broaden the word, I'm trying to broaden it in a sense to the mysticism that's there for all of us.

"But institutions would always have difficulty with mysticism in that sense, because mysticism entails freedom and openness. There are two words that institutions don't like! But, y'know, that's part of reality, and that's what we struggle with."

"Yet isn't that very much a part—inherently, a part—of Celtic roots, the deep connectedness to the Divine in and through Nature, everywhere?"

"I'm not an expert in Celtic Spirituality, Margo. It's very much a part of what is being presented today, this Celtic Spirituality. Now there is another train of thought in Ireland which would suggest that this isn't Celtic Spirituality at all. I've read some very interesting articles by people who would suggest that this is fantasy... Celtic Spirituality. The reality of Celtic Spirituality was a lot more mundane, and also a lot more oppressive and narrow than they are professing. There is a magazine called 'Spirituality' that had a great article, a critique of John O'Donoghue's book (*Anam Cara*) by a Dominican from Scotland on that whole thing. 'Twas fascinating. Now I wouldn't be able to assess where the truth is. But it was a very, very interesting approach to John's writing. Have you liked what John wrote?"

"I have... But then, I felt that he had said what he had really wanted to say, and the rest was sort of a variation on the theme. I didn't finish."

"Many of us didn't finish."

"I found parts of it very lovely..."

"Have you ever heard him speaking?"

"No."

"He's a marvelous speaker. You know, on radio. On some radio station the other morning, for an hour on National Radio, he was on. He is riveting. His voice, his use of language. But in the end you wonder, what did he say? While you're listening to it, you don't... because you're drawn into it. His language is beautiful. It really is. I know John is a fine fellow. But anyway..."

"Coming back to the mystic theme, you know, in Scripture where it talks about the letter of the law and the letter of the..."

"...Spirit..."

"One leads to life and one leads to..."

"Yes. And at the same, I s'pose, we need laws."

"We do."

"There will always be that conflict. But undoubtedly, here in Ireland, we are coming out of a recent tradition where law utterly dominated. The price has to be paid, and it's paid in terms of the anger and the discouragement and everything else that you're meeting. Mmm... interesting times."

"I was with a group of young people yesterday. Sixteen-year-olds, I believe. Some of them were able to start talking, and they said they liked the year they were in, the transition year, because they said they really didn't have a lot they had to be responsible for. Yet the teacher, who was still in the classroom with us, then said that after this year, they had to make a decision about what they want to do with their life. And I said, 'Well, I'm sure they can change their minds, can't they?' And she said, 'Well, not really...' How can you possibly know at age fifteen, sixteen what you're going to do with the rest of your life? I didn't know when I was thirty, forty... I still am not sure."

"Exactly."

"You brought that out in your book as well. How could they know?"

"We have a crazy education system at the moment in Ireland."

"It's not just in Ireland. The kids in America are under undue pressure as well. Yesterday they admitted how apprehensive they are, that now they have to decide what they want to do in the future. And with the exams and the leaving certificates. One young woman said 'it's scary.' At the end of that, I found myself suggesting, putting it in their own language as much as I could, for them to try to think about the things they always loved to do, even when they were younger. Maybe write a list of the things that they loved to do, that gave them joy, and for those times that were rough patches, to go back to that list. A lot of them were very quiet after that. The pressure for these young people is just incredible. What do they have to fall back on? Is the Church there for them?"

"That's right. And often even family isn't great."

"A lot of broken families, separations...The teacher mentioned afterward to me that the mother of one of the girls had called only the day before. The father had just left and that they've separated. She asked the teacher to please watch her girl because she's worried about her."

"The suicide rate is increasing. Very difficult to live with, all the insecurities…"

"But my hope is that there are enough people who care, who are concerned, and even through their very being—whether they're teachers working directly with the children—or writers, priests, or religious, whatever. Somehow, to be able to live their life, our life, as a beacon, a beacon of hope…"

"Yes, in my bad moments I would be very pessimistic about Irish life and Irish society. You know, a lot of other people have said this, that Ireland has been so peculiarly and uniquely Catholic. It doesn't have any other sustaining philosophy or any other sort of moral code, say like Western Europe would have had, say with the Enlightenment or French Revolution time, there would be all sorts of philosophy and morality built around say the French Revolution… liberty, equality, fraternity, and all that sort of thing, which I think is very significant. The English, the British society, which hasn't been particularly religious for a long time… The Church of England has been more a social, maybe unfair to say, more social, but wouldn't have been as strongly

127

and specifically religious as, say, the Catholic Church in Ireland. But Britain has a whole... a sense of decency, a sense of right behavior, a sense of morality. Maybe it was extreme during the Victorian times, but it was a way of living that wasn't specifically religious. It went beyond them and outside of the religious. The people who were not particularly religious would still have this code for which they lived. Ireland has nothing like that. Everything in Ireland is Catholic and Church. So, if you dismantle that, you're in danger of being left with no moral code. And no sense of right behavior. And a society that hasn't got that is lost."

"And that's what I'm sensing... confusion and almost a loss of identity. And my concern is what's left is a vacuum, and then what's going to happen?"

"Oh, that stuff would worry me. A woman came to talk with me the other day, thirty-ish, a very good Catholic upbringing. Quite an intelligent woman, very good job, all that sort of thing. And she began last year rejecting the Church. But she had got herself involved in sort of an Eastern spiritual movement based in Galway city. Now, it was the greatest load of nonsense. It was pitiful. There were all sorts of vague, nice-sounding beliefs, with absolutely no basis in anything. 'Twas a hodge-podge of little bits of Eastern philosophy, but nothing of substance. And here she was, jumping into this lock, stock and barrel, having rejected something that at least has a very sound basis for the Christian belief. Christianity was taught to her reasonably well, and still the Church wasn't bringing her back. She was taking a different path. I thought, 'My God! Out of the frying pan, into the fire.' You see a lot of that, and that's the big danger in Ireland, that people would go...

"And of course, the other thing in Ireland that's becoming a big danger is becoming vastly materialistic. Going back to the schools. The big thing in school now is to get your best possible results in your 'leaving certs.' If you had been here two or three weeks ago, all the talk was of points. The leaving certs results are based on so many points, and you need so many points to get into the different universities. The big thing was, 'Did you get four hundred and fifty points'... to go to Trinity to do medicine, whatever. When we were being educated thirty, forty years ago, there wasn't anything of that hard, personalistic thing. There was more to life than gettin' a big job for yourself. There was the notion of service and there was the idealism... but most of all, being just children. So we are in real danger of becoming materialistic. And whatever the Church of Ireland has to offer, even with all its faults and failures, is better than harsh materialism."

(He smiled.)

"No more questions! Thank you so much..."

"I thank you..."

TONY FLANNERY, C.fgSs.R, was born in Attymon, County Galway, and has been a Redemptorist priest for over thirty years. He has a large following as a preacher and retreat master. His previous publications include 'Keeping the Faith', 'The Death of the Religious Life' and 'From the Inside'.

I never saw them again...

Joan was a woman in her early sixties, well dressed and poised. The setting was once again a garden. We were sitting on a bench and chatting in a relaxed sort of way, both of us very aware of how beautiful the day was. It was very still, no wind...the fragrance of the air so pure, so sweet. The birds were conversing busily with one another up in the branches of nearby cedars. I asked Joan, "From the perspective of being in the Church of Ireland, living in a town where most of it is a Catholic influence, what's that like for you and what was it like growing up?"

"Growing up... I grew up near Dublin, which was a

different scene, I s'pose, because there seemed to be a lot more Church of Ireland people around. And all the parish was in reach of each another, and it was just a good social scene. You grew up on the road, you played with everybody, y'know, it seemed, 'til we went to secondary school, say, about age twelve, ten to twelve. It seemed as if suddenly your friends were who you were in school with, and you just didn't have anything to do with Catholics, until you grew up and went out into the working world, you know. Then you made friends with both sides of the, of the, um… It's not a religious divide, but you know, on both sides of the religions. I must say it was lovely, growing up. But you kept quiet. You didn't sort of push the fact that you were a Protestant particularly, you know; even from the parents' point of view, they didn't want to rock the boat in any way. We had a lovely childhood with the Church, actually. Youth groups and Sunday school and other kinds of clubs and all those sort of things that gave you plenty of activities within your parish… But down here it's a little different, because, well, numbers are smaller.

"We've always got along very well here. I was in the ICA, which is the Irish Country Women's Association. I think I joined it really to meet people when we'd been here awhile. All of them, they were so friendly. They'd like you to join a committee, and they wanted you to be as involved as much as possible. I think I was maybe one of two or three Protestants in the whole big, quite a big, branch. It didn't matter... I haven't found any problems, anyway.

"It was formed years ago. It is really for country people, gives them an outing or an outlet. I enjoyed that for a few years, and eventually I think I was probably the only Church of Ireland person in it, but it didn't really ever worry me. It didn't make any difference."

"The last time I was here, you told a story, I'm sure you could remember, about the day when you were arranging flowers on the altar?"

"Oh, yes.... And the three young boys kind of put their heads around the door, and they wanted to know what place it was, and what church it was, and could they have a look around. And I said they could have a look around for about five or ten minutes or so, and then I'd have to lock up. So when we were going out toward the gate, one of them said, 'But you don't believe in God,' and I said 'Oh, yes, we do.' 'You don't believe in

133

Jesus, do you?' 'Oh, yes, we do.' I could not believe that they were growing up and knowing so little about it and thinking that we didn't believe in the same God as they did. I was amazed at that. It would be within the last five or six years, I would say, because before that we used to hear that the Catholic children were taught not to go near our church. And at one time you would have to get permission to attend a wedding or a funeral, even. But we thought all that had changed. And then it just amazed me that these three lads, they were about ten years of age, asking so many questions, and what was our service like. I said, 'Very, very similar to your own. Why don't you come along now some day and see for yourself?' But of course they didn't..." *(Gentle laugh.)* "So that was a bit of a surprise to me, I must say." *(Long pause.)* "I never saw them again...

"We have had a bit of problem with children going in and vandalizing. I don't think it's just the Church of Ireland they vandalize; I think it's happening in general with any school or church property that we could have quite a bit of trouble. When I saw them coming in, I wondered. But then I just said, 'If you'd like to have a look around, do,' and they had a quick look around, and decided this wasn't too strange, and were happy then to just come out with me."

"You never know, though, when something like that happens, if these children, growing up, someday will remember this incident..."

"They might... they might..."

"Now, some of the questions I've asked of others: what is your relationship with the Church today, what sustains you, what do you find is life-giving? Where do you find God?"

"I could find God anywhere, really, I think. Somewhere like this, the garden. Church is important to me, to go to church. Hopefully fifty Sundays out of fifty-two, I do my best to attend. I find if I miss, I feel I'm losing touch somewhere... it's important to me. And also, in Lent now, when we have Bible studies, I would try to go to those. Yes, I think if I didn't do some of these things, I would slip away. As somebody said, it's a habit maybe, goin' to church. But it's a good habit, and it's very easy to miss a few weeks and say, 'Oh, well, I'm fine, really.' So for me it's important to keep on going because I would hate to slip away from that.

"The rest of the week, well... I do pray. Actually I have set times I pray, in particularly if I have something on my mind, or somebody. I pray where I am, basically. I'm not as good at reading my Bible as I used to be or as I should be, although I do read it from time to time, but can't say it is regular. When I was younger I read it very regularly." *(Sigh.)* "Yes. I think if you—yes, I think wherever—if you have need of Him, He is there for you, isn't He, wherever you look for it. I've always found that, anyway... And He's definitely found in the Scriptures, of course, in the Bible. I will always turn to the Bible if I have a worry or have a problem or something like that. I would be drawn to reading, very often the Psalms, or sometimes just opening at random and finding a verse or two."

I asked Joan what her life has been like.

"I am a mother, but my family are grown up. I did work, only maybe some part-time work, a good many years ago. Lately, I haven't worked outside the home. My mother's living with us now. Just since October. She hadn't been well, so she's come to live with us, and it's working out very nicely. She's very happy, and she's settled in. It's just my husband and myself and herself, and we all fit in very nicely together. There's a nursing home not too far from here. My week would be... a couple of days a week out to see my aunt, and wherever Mom needs to go, I have to take her, basically, because she can't walk very far. We try to fit in a few walks. Other than that, the garden at this time of year takes a lot of time. We have a biggish garden... That's the sort of thing. We're sort of slowing back, I sort of feel now, because my husband is retired and my mother's sitting around a lot of the time. I found I was beginning to sit around. And then I got bored with that, so am getting out and about. I go to an art class once a week, just for enjoyment. And in the summer, I hope to go for a swim a few times in the sea... I like the outdoors."

"Looking back over the years, what kind of perspective would you have now? Would you like to change anything about your life? Is there a sense of fulfillment, would you say you have a sense of well-being in your life?"

"Yes, yes... very happy, really. I don't look back and

say, 'I wish I had had a full-time job,' because I don't, quite honestly. There were two boys very close together, just a year apart. They took quite a bit of raising. And then, after a gap of six years, I had a daughter, which was wonderful! I was quite happy to look after them. A lot of time was taken up, really, taking them places and collecting them and so on. I found that, I don't know, a bit frustrating at times, but it was very fulfilling. My husband and myself were always... great friends. We get on very well and we do quite a lot of things together. Not everything, but quite a few things together. It's been a good life. Very simple, very ordinary life, I suppose. Very happy, really... lucky... we've been blessed."

"It seems that a lot of people these days are longing for a simpler life. Our lives get so complicated, so complex..."

"Well, I found that when I was overly busy, I'd get stressed. It would affect my stomach and everything. So it was easier to just, y'know, say, well, I'll do just so much. I guess we were lucky that my husband's job meant he was able to support the five of us very well, so we didn't have to worry too much about extra money coming in. I grew a few things in the garden and felt that I was contributing that way. Life has been very good. A few holidays here and there, a few weekends away during the year and a fortnight's holiday. You'd look forward to those very much.

"We were away for the month of November this year. We were in Australia and New Zealand and we came home by way of Los Angeles, a couple of days with my cousin there. So that was a real once-in-a-lifetime, long trip. We've not been able to go away for a month. It was a good trip. It was great. Had a wonderful time... Looked up some friends and family along the way."

"Your children... are they married?"

"One's married. One is engaged. We have one grandchild and two more on the way. Our eldest son is living here in town, and the other two are both in England. The married son is in England, and my daughter's engaged... and she's in England as well. We see them a few times a year. We can be there in a few hours on the train. They come over once a year, maybe. That's a new interest, of course, having a new grandchild, and

139

another one due in July, early July, hopefully. Looking forward to that."

"Sounds like a lovely life. I think the trend now is... well, young people seem to want more and more, and there seems to be almost a frenetic over-busyness."

"Yes... yes. I don't know how they can manage if they have children. I think it must be very rushed. I was so pleased that our daughter-in-law gave up work when their baby arrived. She's going to mind him full-time. I'd say she probably would go back to work in maybe five or six years' time. But she just wants to be a 'mom.' And I think my other son's girlfriend, that's all she wants, too, is sort of have a family, and be a housewife and mom. That's her ambition, really, which is great! They both like cooking, which is another point. A lot of the younger ones haven't time to cook! My two sons seemed to have found themselves people who look after them.

"My one son is a marine engineer, and he's working in the dockyard down here, and my other son is in business, he has a business degree. Commerce. He's getting on quite well with a shipping company, but he doesn't go to sea. He's totally office based, and he's very happy with that."

"What did your husband do?"

"He was a marine engineer as well. Came ashore, took a job ashore shortly after we were married. He'd been doing marine engineering, but with boats that were being maintained here rather than going sailing on them."

"So he's not really quite retired yet?"

"He has retired actually, yes, he's finished now. He retired a year ago."

"Is he happy?"

"Yes, he is. Yes, indeed... very."

"Retirement can be a rough time, for both the spouses."

"Yes... He did two years of part-time, just going in three days a week, to ease himself into it. Now I think he

141

wonders how he found time to work, because people keep asking him to do things and take on things. He's taken on quite a few little things, carpentry things, and he's busy. He's very busy. He seems to be enjoying it."

After a rather long pause, I asked Joan if there was anything that she might want to say about the way the Church might be going, what her hopes for the future might be.

"I guess the concern is that you don't see young people coming to church, my own family included. I mean, they've dropped away. Some, you see them coming back, maybe, when their children are of a certain age. But just lately, you see even very few children coming. That's a concern. I feel that they're missing so much. It's sad. That will be a concern... how long can we all keep on doing what we're doing in the Church, and who's going to take over when we're sort of slowing down? And yet, there are a few signs, there are a few young people coming along. If we just keep on believing and hoping that there will be people coming in to carry on what we've been a part of us so long. That's a big concern, I think, that young people don't seem to have the faith anymore. It's sad, isn't it?"

I thanked her for her time.

SOMETIMES A STAR...

oh, you're damned,
oh God, you're damned…

Sean and Carmel are a couple in their late sixties. Sean was the first to say something, being the more talkative one. But Carmel seemed very accommodating, once she had a chance to speak.

"Since I grew up, there's that kind of 'fed up' with the Church. Even before that, I'd say, people, they'd get fed up with the Church. They were already losing their faith, they had a crisis of faith. Nine o'clock Mass in the morning, you had to go to confession once a week. You

145

had to do this, you had to do that. Every time you looked around, it was a sin. So I think that the older generation of priests and bishops have an awful lot to answer for, in my opinion. Because they kind of made the whole church-going thing, and God, a kind of thing like when you'd get a big stick. I'm sixty-nine years old, I'm sorry, I think back a good bit. It didn't harm me. Bishops, the whole lot of 'em, no matter what they do, no matter what the bishop says or what he's going to do, if you really think about your faith, you stick by the man who died there. You stick by Him. Like we had a scandal with a bishop. How many more that we never heard of, that's possibly still going on?

"You could come up along to retreats and missions throughout the country in a cathedral or another place. You have a retreat for a week. The priests would be up there on the pulpit, and you were damned, you were damned. Everything was wrong. If you went out with a girl, and you kissed a girl, that was a mortal sin. Now I mean, how they ever thought that people could want to find out about each other, learn about each other and get married. I don't know how these guys were thinking. But they thought everything was a sin. If you put your hand on top of a girl's shoulder, if ya gave her a quick

146

hug... a mortal sin. So it was a strict thing, in the Catholic Church in Ireland. I don't know what was wrong. And Confession. All a matter of interpretation. You know, what always struck me very forcibly at that time when I was growing up... impurity. Impurity was the greatest sin you ever committed. You could go out— this is my interpretation, I might have it wrong, but it doesn't matter—you could go out and kill somebody, go straight into confession and turn to the priest and say, 'Father, pray for me, I just murdered a man, or a woman...' and the priest says, 'Don't do it again. Dear Lord, this is very serious...' And if you went to a priest, and said, 'I was out with my girlfriend, I opened her blouse and I put my hand on her breast...' 'Oh, you're damned, oh God, you're damned'..."

(He hit the table with his fist.) "Ah, yes, that is a fact... that is a fact. So, where will we be going from all that? Now a lot of people coming on, the younger generation coming up, will be begin to say, 'This is all bog wash...'

"Back to the situation with the priests themselves. They must have never studied the Bible. And theology, call it what you like, all the theology in the world is no good, unless you have a big stick with you. I think per-

147

sonally, they did not study the Bible. In the Bible, when the woman was taken, caught in adultery, they brought her in front of everybody... a disgrace. And what did Christ say to her? 'Go, sin no more.' Just go and sin no more. He didn't say, 'How many times did you commit adultery, why and how...' Just that she was sincere, she was about to be stoned. They would stone people at that time. I remember reading in my Bible study! But there you have it, right? Why were all the priests coming on? Who was teaching 'em all this fire and brimstone fear of the Lord stuff? The younger priests now are different. Y'see, the authority of the Church was dominant, and began to slip, and slip, and slip. And now, I'm sad to say, as many as ninety-five percent of people in Ireland don't respect the authority of the Church in Ireland. 'Tis sad, right? That's my honest opinion. And a lot can be blamed on the people themselves. You see, the priests and bishops were up on pedestals for so many years... They were just representing God. They are the same as any other man.

"When you're born, you're either male or female, man or woman. You grow up, you might become a nun, you might become a priest, you might eventually become a bishop. But you're a human being, with all the faults that we all have. Is temptation any different because you're a bishop? But who are we to judge then! 'Oh, we won't go to that church.' We go to church because of Christ! If all the bishops went out with all the women in the world, that's not your problem, it's their problem! And then I think in latter years now, with Ireland booming economically, everybody— *everybody*—we're all affected in some way with this... the rat race. 'You must have a better car than I have.' It was mentioned on the radio, on television... during the week, on the news. Voluntary organizations are finding it very difficult to get people to give a handout. Nobody wants to do *anything* without getting paid. And that is a sad thing in Ireland. People, their time is so valuable. They must go ahead with, well, call it what you like, I s'pose... socializing, going out, seven days a week, three hundred and sixty-five days a year... They're going somewhere. And that's sad. And if we get any more prosperous, there'll be fewer people thinking of God. We all get a touch of it, like... But I think now in Ireland today that's what's wrong. Greed has taken over. Well, not everybody, you can't generalize. But, oh God, an awful lot of the population.

"I pity the youngsters growing up. They're having children, not getting married. I suppose I blame the government in a lot of that, because if you don't get married in Ireland and you live together, if you really decide, 'Right, we'll shack up together. You keep your job, I'll keep my job.' You pay less tax. So, there are the incentives, 'Don't get married.'

"Now our daughter, she has a small B&B, running a small B&B. It was our place, but we left that to them, and we went to the smaller house. But having said that, sometimes she comes in and says, 'We're trying to make ends meet. We're paying the mortgage, we're paying for this and we're paying for that, and we're paying for our children going to school.' And so-and-so up the road, she had three children, she knows the father of one, and she's getting handouts left and right. But she can get everything. Even for driving lessons, the state will pay. Y'know, and all this is, is, turning people away from God. Where does God fit into all of this? But they don't think of it. Now, someone's gone off with some other fella's wife and vice versa. And if you say anything to them, now you might just be having a general conversation, and you might say, 'But how do you feel about this?' 'I was never so happy in a physical way.' But d'ya see my point? God isn't mentioned. Isn't that wrong? In other words... Jack and Mary, they're happy as larks. Their families, they left behind. A and B are living together, and C... and there's a child born in the middle. And they went around to have the baby christened, in the Catholic Church. And the sacristan comes out, they were very friendly with him, and they laugh when they come up. And they said, 'This is the mommy, and this is the daddy.' The daddy belonged to the other children! In time, brothers and sisters will be getting married or they'll be living together. So that's just it, my interpretation of the whole scene in Ireland today. We have very good Christian people, the young people are very good Christians, but as to going into a church, they aren't there. There was a young priest just this morning, he makes his point. And why not, he's quite entitled to have a point, if he wishes. He's trying to mix with the younger people, maybe trying to give them God through himself. God uses everybody in different ways, as we know."

"Sean, may I ask, what keeps you going?"

"I pray every day. I talk to Him every day like I'm talking to you. But by going to church, you're going in to receive Him. So why not come get Him into your soul every day and He'll keep you going. Now probably you'll have a rough patch, and you might forget to go to Mass or the alarm clock didn't go off. I'm a reader, and I'd be reading. Not every Sunday. We rotate. But for some unknown reason, the week that I'm on for Mass to read, of all the mornings, all that week, I stayed in bed. I slept on. And if I hadn't to do it… well, I know you don't have to, but you do it. But, like, the week that you're not on, then you find you're awake at the dawn, bright and cheerful, you jump up in bed. But is that the devil, I say?

"I think the whole problem in Ireland today is that people are losing their faith because of materialism. And the world has gotten so small now, with telecommunications, that it's proving this and proving that, and people are being affected by it all. 'Tis sad. 'Are you happy? Wouldn't you love to have this?' I don't know… I remember a woman asking if I won the four million lotto, what would I do? 'I don't know.' But she said she assumed that I'd look after my family and give so much to charity. And she said, 'At the end of the day, you wouldn't have enough, because what you're telling me, you'll be giving it away to such an extent when you get to the end of the list, oh, look, we've got nothing for Johnny... it's all gone.' Then she said, 'We pray to the Lord that we'll win the lottery.' Oh, dear Lord...

"But maybe that's it. People are hoping for this, this dream... the dream that they have. Most people today, its money, this lottery thing. To be a millionaire. And drugs, people will kill for money for drugs. It's greed. Deep down, the drug barons are greedy men and women who are just catching youngsters into this terrible way. And the youngsters get so caught up in this, they'll kill for money for drugs. I'm not judging these people; these are just some of my thoughts...

(Sean continued...)

"I suppose in the end, you have to 'take up your cross.' Some people think the cross is sickness... it could be a terrible bout of, God forbid, cancer or whatever, that the Lord might send your way. The cross, too, can be that people are saying, 'Oh, you're a goodie-goodie,' or something. 'You're a do-gooder, goin' into the church.' That's a cross too. That's been tested. Our forefathers would kill for their faith. And at other times, possibly laughing at youngsters... Maybe that's why a lot of

153

youngsters get fed up, peer pressure and all. And they just don't go to church, which is sad.

"Television. Of course you could be blaming everything, but it's within yourself, I think. Television would have a lot to do with influencing people. People are even hooked on it. That's fine. Time's a very precious thing. 'Tis the way you use your time. But that's it, really. If you give your time to people. But unfortunately, like in Ireland, we're losing it. The older people still have it, but then the older people have been very upset by all the changes.

"The other day, after Mass, we were standing there by the bookshop. We were there with an older man. He's the nicest person you ever met. He'll come up to you after Mass, and he'll make you feel ten feet tall. He's ninety-two years old, and he looks like a little boy. And he's always cutting up... Three of us went down to the local pub for a pint one evening. It looked like an English comedy, three fellas, retired. And he would make us laugh... to do you for a tonic! Now he would say, 'Was I all right last night?' He doesn't drink at all! He has such a fantastic outlook on life. He's ninety-two years old, maybe ninety-three now. But he lifts everybody who comes in contact with him. Jack wanted to get a Mass card signed. He saw a young man come out who lit the candles and got the book ready. So I said, 'Jack, they must have ordained him, and we didn't know it.' We had a bit of fright. We thought he was the altar boy! 'I know,' he said, 'I went to get a Mass card signed...' And this is another thing. Now I think the priests would begin to think this is a good thing, I dunno, I feel, oh, I don't know, I don't like it. 'This little boy came in to the sacristy, marched in to say 10 o'clock Mass, with a white T-shirt.' And Jack now, a man of ninety-two years, he's seen an awful lot of changes, which he doesn't like and he'll tell you so. And he said, 'This fella, he kind of wandered up.' You see, they're renovating the church. He thought he was actually one of the workers. And he signed the Mass card! And Jack said, 'I told him,' he said, 'put Father down there... Father, Father,' hitting the table with his finger. Because the priest could just get a Mass said for so-and-so, and sign, 'Paddy O'Malley,' or whatever. 'Put *Father* Paddy O'Malley!' Paddy O'Malley could be the painter, the plumber... he could be anybody!

"These are the things that mean a lot, especially to the older people, and I think it's only right, they should. But nowadays, in seminaries they're being taught today

155

that they're going out to preach the Word of God, so mix with the people, dress like the people. You're just one of them. Now when our Lord was around, what they saw was not so much that he was dressed up as a priest. Because obviously back then, a priest didn't wear a collar as we know it. But they knew, because they could see, there was love flowing out from Him. He was around, healin' people. He didn't have to be wearing a special garment. You don't need special garb. If you do somethin' for a person, do it... and carry on with life. But you'd still like to see a priest with some identification. I mean, what if I would go around to some person, and say, 'I bless you now, and I'll hear your confession.' They wouldn't have a clue if I were a priest or not! And that's it, it's happening. And some young people, young priests, are being very cute, and they take advantage of others...

"Well, that's my story now. I'm not trying to judge. A lot of damage has been done. And the sad thing about that, especially with older people, I think; they're becoming very disillusioned. During the period we were growing up, the churches were packed. You'd bow down to the priests, you'd kiss the bishop's ring, and his feet, and whatever else. And all this was going on... they had their affairs, and all this going on. There were priests and bishops fathering children. That was all going on during what was thought as the 'golden years' of the Church. At the same time, God was breathing out on them... That's what matters now. And what will be left will be a glorious Church. Again, we mightn't see it, but it will come...

"There was a man, a chap we knew, and he was talking one day about the past. They were just starting the dockyard here, and there was work, there was work coming. And one man said, 'Jimmy, what do you think of the jobs coming? Wages will be good, and people will be able to do some little bit better than what they're doin' now.' And Jimmy said, 'Yes, I agree with you. It's grand to see young men being taken off the streets. They're getting married, and they can raise their family, and they'll have money coming in, earning their keep.' But he said, 'I hope the day will never come when Ireland will get too prosperous that they'll lose their faith...' Not long ago, a fella said that to me in chapel, and he said, 'Go to Mass, and do the best you can. But what about all the people who don't go to Mass, but they're still believin', they pray to God and talk to Him.' And I said, 'Sure, why not.' Sure it's important to go to Mass when you can, and receive the Lord. But why not

157

ask the Lord for help, small jobs, big jobs, at the shop. When you have to cope with somethin', even simple things. Well, why not talk to Him? Like we're talking now... You don't have to be on your knees all day long, sayin' prayers. Why don't we just take Him as He is? 'I'm with you 'til the end of time,' He said.

But, that's, that's me...

"Now, about the faith in Ireland... To my mind, it's sad. Apart from the Church, all governments, the ministers there, the prime ministers and all... they all went down different paths. It's all about money. And that doesn't help young people, especially. They're not going to church, they're unhappy, they can't get their act together. Well, what's going to happen? Same with politicians... rotten to the core, I think. It's callin' a spade a spade. And yet, we're supposed to look up to these people as our leaders. There's so much publicity. Whether it be true or false, then, that's another side of the story. I wouldn't believe what I read in the papers. You just don't know the facts, especially when they're downing somebody, which is frightening. I must admit, 'tis frightening..."

(Sean turned to his wife, who had been sitting there,

quietly listening.) "What's that book we have at home, Father Tom...uh..."

(Carmel answered:) "Oh, Flannery, Tony Flannery..."

(Sean continued.)

"'*From the Inside.*' An excellent book. We have brushes or run-ins, call it what you like, with bishops. But I think the bishops got the message from him in his book. He made some brilliant points in that book. I'll probably read it again. But he's still writing, I presume. Is he, is he in Ireland? He's down in Limerick, isn't he? A Redemptorist. But he had mentioned now in that book about the missions, and the Redemptorists. Oh, how they could talk...

"All I can say is, believe in the man who died here for us. And we need Mass—and to take God into your soul—and it keeps ya going. Sure, you can be a very good Christian. Even growing up like me, there could be a friend of yours who died, who was in the Protestant church. You weren't supposed to go! Now they are Christian people making their way to God. They're on their way, and they believe in God. They're fine people, and we were taught you shouldn't go, and you shouldn't do this and you shouldn't do that. Nowadays, we're fully in and out, like last Sunday, we sang in the Protestant Church. Ya see, it was the choir…   Last year we were asked to do it and we did it again this year. There's nothing wrong with that. We have different beliefs, particularly with the Eucharist, y'know. So we're Christian. Grand. Catholic… It shouldn't make a difference. We believe that Christ is on the altar. I don't know what the Protestants believe in the Eucharist. But they still believe that it is the Body of Christ, in their own way. I have great respect for the Protestants, and the Protestant minister here is a lovely man. In fact, he conducted some of the Bible studies we were going to with one of our local priests. He was a Bible historian and it was great. He was bringing it to life. You could see the countryside with the Holy Man… you could see. 'Twas a great help. It was like Christ was around, y'know? Like in Thessalonians, I often wondered, they'd walk miles and miles to get to different places. And I was thinking, they must be very fit! In those days they didn't have cars.

"And another book, *'Miracles Do Happen.'* She's brilliant. What's her name? She knew one of our friends, a priest. He was kind of our spiritual director and our helper in our work. And so one day she asked him to join her for a cup of tea in a pub, so he said 'sure, yeah, why not.' They sat at a table, and she said, 'Jesus is nearby, sittin' with us. Jesus is sitting with us this whole time.' And he thought she was losing it, big time! But that man said he could feel the presence of somebody sitting beside 'em. So he said, 'What is Jesus wearing?' 'He has on a white suit...' She described the suit! He could say nothing.

"But people don't invite Him. A simple thing like that. I mean, that's the way you should do it. We don't do it all the time, but maybe half the time... we genuinely invite Him. Another friend of ours... oh, what you'd hear if you had a tape recorder in the pub, especially on a Friday night! He asked me, 'Do you invite Jesus up now if you're comin' up for a pint?' and I say, 'Oh, sure... He gave us drink to enjoy.' And he said, 'Would you?' 'Yeah, and I invite Him when I go for a drive in the car. I drive the car with me and Jesus Christ.' And I said, 'You can do that too!' But why not? Bring Him up with you for a pint! There's nothing wrong with that at all. Behind the scenes, you can invite Him when you enjoy yourself, when you're with your friends. Y'know?

161

Just say, 'Let's go for a pint!' Well, that's enough for now..." *(Laughter.)*

Carmel wanted to say a few things.

"Well, you see, the point I would like to make is, y'know, I really believe that you can't have yesterday and you can't have tomorrow. So you have today. What's happened yesterday or what's happening tomorrow, there's nothing we can do about it. So we only have today. Everything's changing. But it's the same with Mass. You have your Mass; you make the best of it. I'll never forget... I went out for lunch one day with a priest. I was so conscious of him being a priest, being at the table with me. My lunch nearly choked me! Whereas, if I was talking to a normal person, which he is, I agree... but if he were just in ordinary clothes. He was just stickin' out like a sore thumb. It changed all my ideas about priestly clothes after that. I really felt if that man had worn just ordinary clothes, like I was dressed in and everybody else is dressed in, we wouldn't have been kind of looking at him. We would have treated him like an ordinary person. It made such a difference! I really totally changed my point of view on that. Whereas before, I would have said, 'He should be wear-

162

ing priestly clothes and a nun should be all dressed in a habit and all that.' I mean, I see you now as a person because you're dressed in ordinary clothes, and I can get to know you better as a person rather than, 'Oh, she's a nun... you must be very nice to her.' It totally changed my thinking. We all change our ideas after the years. Now a priest, he is just a person first. God chose his vocation. Like in Bridge McKenna's book—I love her, really—she made the point, like she said God spoke to her one night. And He said to her, 'Bridge, you will have to speak my Word. Speak my Word.' He never changed... We're judgin' Him and we're criticizin' Him, but He never judges us. He never does. And He made me as me, and He made Sean as himself. And I can't be him and he can't be me anymore than I can't be you, and you can't be me. And if you really be like that in your life, you'll be a much happier person, and a healthier person. You can really only be yourself. And please yourself! Well, I'd be trying to say, 'I'll be nice now for her, or I'll be really nice for her now today.' Well, I mightn't be nice to you at all! I might be actually annoyin' you! Well, I'd not be being me then. But if I'm being happy being me, then the truth will be there. But I'm happy being myself, and I'm goin' to give it to

163

somebody else then. Y'know? That's the way I feel..."

(Sean responded.) "I'd agree with you, sayin' that. Whether you become a bishop, a priest, a Pope... it doesn't matter. You're a human being *first*. And a human being 'til the day you die. That's it. So if you're a priest, or get married or don't get married, or become a nun, a brother, a monk down at Mallory, it's just another part of your life, of me and you. You can't be anybody else. But like, people should accept that we're human beings, to cope as a human being. We can make errors as a human. You can't be livin' your life to please everybody else; if you do, you're in a bad state. It's just impossible. And y'know, as you go through life, experience should teach you that at the very first... you just can't please everyone.

"Well, we probably gave you enough to think about, huh?

"More than enough, believe me! Thank you, Sean and Carmel..."

a new springtime...

Sister E appeared to be a very spirit-filled, energetic woman in her late thirties. She had a way about her that was no-nonsense, let's get to the point, and get on with it! She is a Sister of Mercy. We met over a cup of tea, sitting outside at a small table with chairs. It was a beautiful day, clear and mild, with a softness in the air. Carillon bells from a nearby cathedral could be heard, the sound quietly wafting over the town.

"Now, Margo, you asked, 'What is it like to be in the Church in Ireland today?' Well, it has its concerns, and it has its expectations. And I s'pose with the beginning of a new millennium, or the end of every century, there's

165

always been a dark time, and one could say this is a very dark chapter in the Church in Ireland in its history. But nevertheless, we're beckoned on, especially by the promise of Christ, and we have it in Matthew's Gospel, when He said, 'I'll be with you always, yes, 'til the end of time.' That's reaching on into the next millennium. We bring with us our fears and our hopes. There are many things, too, in the Church in Ireland today that give us new hope, fresh hope—as the writer Christopher Frye says, 'Thank God our time is now.' We're living in the 'now' time. And he even mentions, he gives the hint—and that was way back in the early part of the twentieth century—gives a hint of the dark history as well, when one comes up to face this everywhere, never to leave us, until we take the furthest leap that we have ever taken. Enterprise is now so fine, so fine an enterprise... a movement into God. And that's where we come from in our Irish Church. We come from a very strong root in this, and awareness that God is present. And that's symbolized in the Celtic design that you see everywhere in Ireland—in the tombstones, in the crosses, in drawings, in the Book of Kells; that interweaving of lines. So God, too, weaves in and out of our lives, very much part of the stuff our life is made of. We bring that with us from our forefathers, from way back even when Patrick arrived in Ireland in the early fifth century. He found here a very strong sense of spiritual hope. It was extraordinary for him to just pick up a shamrock and to teach the people a little bit more doctrine, that God is 'Three and One,' the whole Presence of the Trinity. And that sign of the Cross, which we see... Modern teenagers in all kinds of modern apparel, we see them automatically sign themselves with that Cross when there's danger near, or when a funeral passes by, or passing a Church... That's still part of our Irish heritage, thankfully, being carried on by a lot of young people, maybe not by every young person, but by a lot of young people... a sense of appreciation that there is this strong relationship between us and Father, Son, and Spirit.

"Recently we had that lovely Legend of Light— which I didn't see, but I can just sense what it was all about, and enter it as if I were there. Where you had the dark and the light, and where you had the cry, and where you had the sense that there was some deep Presence there in the darkness and in the coming of Light. That was down in Cashel, and was very masterfully done by our modern composer, Liam Lawton, and his team. And Tim Fouhy here, who started the Parish team. So, light

167

and fire have been very much strong symbols to us in our faith. Yesterday I was at a Profession ceremony of a Sister, a nurse in Mercy Hospital in Cork. It was held in the Church of the Missionary Fathers. The whole entrance was bringing up the light first, and then the fire. That was done to movement. Four young girls did a very, very beautiful dance right up the church, bringing the light and bringing the fire, before ever the ceremony began, and hinting back that our journey of our Christian faith began in baptism. And it was being deepened yesterday with the Sister giving of herself to the Mercy family internationally. We had many people there, some Mercy Sisters from Peru... South America. One man, the priest at the altar, had ministered in Peru as well. So it was a great sense of our story being part of everybody's story. Just thinking of those great symbols; the ceremony wouldn't have been right without them.

"So light, and fire, and water, too, are symbols that continue to speak to us in our world today. All those wells that were part of our Irish life, that quenched our thirst, that helped with washing of the clothes. All those wells are going to be opened up and these places have become places of pilgrimage now. Holy wells.

I think the whole sense that life, the way we live life,

168

despite the Celtic Tiger... that that's very much woven into the life of God, or should be. And that's constant, that we're just working at it and trying to keep going. I think music and art and literature are great helpers in that whole endeavor. So we encourage the Irish musician and the Irish poet... There are many Irish musicians now, young people. I think that's going to keep the faith alive for them as well. Our faith is part of the ordinary, everyday humdrum. It's not separated from it. That's what makes our Christianity in Ireland more livable. So, it's a good time to be, to be in Ireland..."

"I've heard great concern that many people are not going to church, especially among the younger generation."

"Well, I feel sorry, but y'know, goin' to church is not everything. I know it's very important. It is the center of the Christian life. But that doesn't mean, the fact that they're not goin' to church doesn't mean that they aren't spiritual or that they aren't searching for God, or that God isn't meaningful to them. It's certainly not the situation. And I think we have to respect where they're at. And certainly, when there's celebration—like what I was at yesterday, the three-hour celebration—there were a lot of young people there. When it's meaningful, and when it engages them, they do go. So, maybe all the fault is not on the side of the young people. Maybe all of us, just that bit older, need to do a bit more reflection. And I don't think they're looking for something high-powered. Young people love the Taize experience of the Eucharist. I think all of us need to put more thought into this. We need to engage them a lot more, from being passive spectators—which was everybody's role in the past—to being actively involved in offering that great worship to the Father, through Jesus, and the Spirit. I know there is a concern, and I'm sure if I was a parent, I'd be concerned too. But I think it's not all negative. It could force, it could force those of us who still go to worship to make it more creative and more meaningful for everybody."

"Here we are in a new millennium. Would you have any words of encouragement for the people in Ireland? You speak of being in a dark time, but hopefully some of these words that are being said now will be available for those who might be floundering or discouraged. And there's even some bitterness, and anger..."

"Yes. Yes. And that's understandable too. But that's part of the pain of being human. There have been injustices. People have been marginalized. But I think we have the wherewithal now through all kinds of human therapies, to help us find our place. Our Pope (John Paul II) was all the time talking about the dignity of the human person. And being a philosopher, he had a great grip on that whole sense of... that each one is so important in the eyes of God. That goes back again to the whole equality that baptism gives us. As far as words of encouragement, I find them in Scripture. Yahweh *does* care for His people. Looking right through the Bible, this is nothing new. This morning I was reading the Book of Lamentations. It's the whole series of people bearing the burden of pain and injustice, and really being angry with God. There are three lovely lines to this thinking:

'Yahweh has not forgotten you.
The favors of Yahweh are not all past...
Every day they are renewed.'

"The fact that we are in a dark history now shouldn't make us think that God holds us in disfavor. Because

171

His favors are not passed. Each morning they are renewed. They're there for the taking, each day, through the power of the Spirit. And I think the more we make our exploration into God, the more hope we find there. Maybe we've explored more into hierarchy of power... which *dis*-empowers people. But certainly the Word can bring something new in each one of us. It's all happening, through the power of the Spirit at work in our world today, the Spirit that keeps our world green... the greening of the human person.

"So there is infinitely great hope. I think that's the whole gesture of opening doors at the dawn of the millennium. Let in this new Spirit, this new creation that will grace our world and is there for the taking. So, if we can leave the rest behind. We can cling onto it, too. I think humankind has an infinite capacity to rise above the past. And the Irish people have. They've done it all the time. Back in the Famine, they went to America, Australia, New Zealand, to create a better future for themselves. And our cathedral that we hear chiming out now... all those who had to leave Ireland sent the money home to build it. It is a pride and joy of our country. So, I would go to the Scriptures and say, 'Be not afraid...'

"I think as a nation, even internationally, we're going to be more mystical. We will be capable of grasping that beckoning that we get from our Creator God. If we can leave aside some of the tags of riches, of worldly riches. That's the challenge, really. But I have great hope. It's going to be a new springtime, and we all know what it's like in the springtime. New life, new energy... There's new awakening. I think if it happens for me, that means it's going to happen for somebody else. We have that power within us, and all those positive vibes that can awake in others. That's what's happening to me, so it's nice to be looking forward to a new springtime."

SOMETIMES A STAR…

a misadventure, or unknown causes...

Seamus was in his late twenties. He was engaging in his conversation, and appeared to be very comfortable talking with me. He seemed to be quite sensitive, especially about the topic he was talking about. It took some courage to address the issue here... On one of my previous visits, Seamus asked if anyone had said anything about suicide.

"In a lot of cases here in Ireland, it's a problem in general, it's a problem with youth... extra pressure with exams, parents putting extra pressure on them. Maybe

175

they should've kicked themselves, or put pressure on themselves and done better to get what they really want to do. You want to be a doctor, so you have to have so many points in the leaving certs. If you don't do that, if you don't get the points and major in that, forget it. It's not just in poorer areas... people of all kinds.

"My aunt, six years ago, committed suicide over a marriage problem. She had split up with her husband, but she couldn't accept that the split took place, even after he went out with another woman. What happened in her case was that—for me, dealing with it, how would you say, experiencing a suicide case—she appeared very happy. She had a son, fourteen, at home. He was deaf and dumb. She loved him dearly, like she'd done every-thing with him. At the time it happened, the split, we all seemed to rally around her. And looking back on it now, I think it made her problems slightly worse, because people split up every day of the week. People who are married for twenty, thirty years, or two years, three years, whatever it is. People split up and they get divorced, whatever. It happens every day of the week. In the case with us—we're a very close family—everyone got around her. I didn't know it had happened at first. I wasn't living at home. I would be home for a weekend.

"When I arrived home that week, the first thing I heard was about my aunt, and that she was down with my other aunt, just down the field. So I went down, and I met her and I hugged her and we talked for a while. I think by everyone getting around her, we made it seem like it was a huge deal, instead of something to be getting over on her own. But at the same time, she couldn't give out everything to us. She was holding an awful lot back in. And in a lot of cases of suicide, it is actually planned. Suicide is actually planned. It's very seldom a spur-of-the-moment thing that happens. What she'd done was... She had been very upset—I think it was a Monday or a Tuesday, I don't remember what day it was—but on the morning of the day she committed suicide, she went around everywhere, the old places that she had been; the place she went to school first, the place where she got married... went to places like that. At the same time, met everyone, met everyone in all the family, where she had gone every day, and told everyone that she had decided to get on with life and forget about him and put the whole thing behind her. And about three hours later, after she had talked with my dad and said that in a very positive manner, she had the car all taped up, a pipe coming through the exhaust of the car, and she died…

"I'm not blaming the family for rallying around her, but I think we made the problem much bigger than what it actually was. You've got that? Maybe in the back of her mind she was going to do it anyway. I think if we just said break-ups happen every day, and get on with it. I know it sounds very harsh, but it's, it's reality, basically…"

(After a few moments of silence, Seamus continued.)

"A few years ago, I did a workshop on suicide. There is a new National Council. There were groups within this new council, different workshops on different things, coming together. Five hundred young people—teenagers, between the ages of sixteen and nineteen, twenty. Obviously students, all students. And they discussed their problems, they discussed what views they had on politics, drugs… everything. Broad spectrum. So, myself and two other friends, we decided to have a workshop on suicide, because there had been so many teenage suicides in our area. We had to grasp as much information as we could about suicide. We met psychologists, psychiatrists. I don't think there was a bereave-

178

ment group. But there was a group of people helping others get over families left behind, and trying to get over that, and how not to explain yourself or explain anyone else.

"We met various people like that in our research into how to approach this. What struck me was, in that age group from sixteen to twenty, an awful lot of young girls were under more pressure than boys. But various people I spoke to... none of them came up and said, 'Hey, I'm thinking of committin' suicide.' But they had this thing in their mind, you would know... it probably had crossed their minds upon occasion. In other words, it's deep stuff, it's a very tough thing to handle. And it's not something people talk about freely. Not too many actually die after they attempt it, but I would think males actually do commit suicide between those ages. It's scary. But they were talking about the reasons behind it all, the pressures of college, the pressures of doing your exams at school. The information we were given was... if you have a lot of stress, do your best to talk about it, be open with your family. Always look for help in any situation, no matter how bad it is, look for help; what people to approach. If you can't talk to your family, talk to someone that you can trust. Probably the

179

best of all is to talk to a stranger. I thought that a bit strange the first time I heard it, but it's actually true. Like you can be walking in the park and meet someone and start talking...

"This happened in conversation with a friend, and when I said it to her, she said, 'Maybe you're right.' And I mentioned it to a psychiatrist, and he agreed whole-heartedly, but he said to me, he genuinely said to me, that he never told anyone to do that. But he said he might try it in the future. Y'know, if it's a priest, a nun, someone you may feel could be a priest—can, well... I think with the culture we have here in Ireland, talking to a priest, it's like confession. You can tell him anything, but you can't tell him you're renouncin' God. Perhaps it's the same with a nun.

"With males, between the ages of twenty-five and thirty-five, it's a common age when they consider taking their lives. And in men again, between the ages of forty-five and fifty. Now, why then is this, you don't know. Well, the twenty-five and thirty-five ages, young men, like myself. I'm twenty-six now. I'm startin' out, I hope to get married next year. I'll have a mortgage, extra pressures than I've had before... like feeding the kids and keeping them happy. Y'know, extra pressure. Never had

180

to do that before. It would be easy to get to a place where you can't cope anymore. Forty-five to fifty... it could be a range of different things with men. With women, it could be menopause. It could be hormones. It could be a constant being afraid of the world..."

"What do you think can be done in the future? Do you think it's going to get any better, or is it going to get worse?"

"Y'see, it's a situation that I think you can find in any person's life. One thing is you can publicize a lot more, but how do you publicize suicide? Perhaps, what could happen is the more you talk about it, the more people will be aware of it and say more what's on their mind. If someone is having struggles or a person talks about being under pressure, you know that maybe suicide is on their mind. Or if a person is in trouble of any kind, you know that maybe they're thinking about suicide. I think talking about suicide should start at an earlier age, perhaps fourteen and fifteen-year-olds in school. Just give them insight into what suicide actually is, how wrong it is, and how people suffer... the ones left behind. I mean, personally I've seen that. I think that by

181

doing that, if someone gets depressed or is under pressure, and if we reflect back to what that person was saying,   that would be the only knowledge we would have of suicide. We may just think of something that person said, a story he may have told, or family he left behind. Perhaps it is a hereditary problem...   We need to talk more about this subject, and experts would agree... Talking to people, and to let people know that suicide isn't the only way out, and that there's something to live for."

"What do you think is the major cause of depression?"

"The causes are so varied. Splits in relationships, pressures at work, pressures in school...   Nowadays people can take money freely from the bank. Well, not freely, but very low interest rates. You may be stable in your work, but yet a long way from the bank and building a house. And the pressures of paying all of that back. You never had to do that before... It can be loneliness, not being able to relate to people, not being able to communicate properly. Social. Perhaps a young man who is overweight or underweight... self-conscious of how they look, and it gets to their feelings. Other people would be mocking them or whatever. That's wrong as well, but it happens."

"What about depression. It's not exactly the same thing as suicide, but it's connected. Is it as common?"

"They are connected, but they're only connected with cases of people who are previously maybe diagnosed as being depressives. But in my research on suicide, depression was a major cause. But depression came from something. Depression's not something you can catch from another person!"

"I know what you're saying. Depression can have different causes, and often its biochemical. Or maybe the disintegration of a relationship, a loss of a job, expectations in school..."

"Exactly. That kind of thing. And some people can be naturally depressed. For so many people, it's so many different things. There's no actual legal term for 'suicide.' It would normally be referred to as, perhaps, a 'misadventure,' or 'unknown causes'...

"I didn't actually understand this, but a psychiatrist told me that a person committing suicide, at the point of committing suicide—whether it be shooting, or jumping off a bridge, or taking an overdose—at the point of committing suicide, that person is sane. Where, leading up to it, it's an insane thing to do. That's the actual controversy. And it's amazing how someone can be really upset, depressed, and all of a sudden, everything's perfect and they're so focused on what they're going to do. I guess with my aunt, she was so focused that day and seemed so... Like, she made everyone happy and seemed like she was getting on with her life. And yet she planned that all along..." *(Long pause.)* "It's very sad for the people that are left behind.

"But I think for people who attempted suicide and never actually, well... who didn't succeed. It's great for the family, but for them, what happens afterwards? This is why people try to commit suicide over and over. From what I can see, these people will not be able to do anything anymore. If someone tried to commit suicide, people know that it is probably in the back of their minds... There are a lot of people who attempt suicide who don't actually go through with it, who are maimed for life..."

"The whole thing is very sobering, just the idea of it. Most people don't want to talk about it, but they may worry about this kind of thing, and don't want to admit there's so much of it."

"Everyone, at some time in their life, is going to come under stress. I'm not saying everyone will think of committing suicide, but at some point they may think, 'I wish it was all over.' I mean, I'm speaking truthfully, and I think its deep down, when they find themselves really down and out. I think if people knew about it from an early age... and when I say an early age, I mean an age when they can understand their feelings and fears. You're not goin' to start preachin' to children who are three or four years of age. I think the ages between fourteen or fifteen, around there. They're coming into adulthood, they're about to become adults. They're more independent, they're going to be more socially active with other people. That's where I think the problem can be met."

"What if, let's say, a friend of yours confided in you and said, 'I really don't want to live any longer,' what would you say? What would you say to them? What if I

185

said to you, 'Seamus, I don't see any reason why I want to live any more'?"

"The first thing I would say to you is, I'd ask you why. I'd question you, the reasons why... I think I would go back to the people you're leaving behind, the domestic scene. I think if it was a personal friend, I would talk to you the same. I would try to get the person not to do it. I think I would say, 'why, why?' I would ask lots of questions. Maybe a person would say, 'I had a row with my parents.' Actually, last year, a person I knew was thinkin' about committing suicide. I felt really terrible. There was a split-up in a relationship. She didn't want to cope... It was spur of the moment. All I could say was, 'It happens every day... I'd love to be your friend.' I was so scared. We went for a long walk, and I remember I stayed with her that night. The following day she was in much better spirits. She was fine, basically. Well, not fine. She was very upset... and so was I."

(There was a moment of quiet, then Seamus continued.) "Actually, I'd love to be one of those people who would go and talk to those who were fourteen or fifteen."

"You mentioned before that maybe a professional

186

person might go and talk with them, like a psychologist or a psychiatrist. And when you said that, it crossed my mind, y'know, I wonder if a younger person closer to their age would be better, and not necessarily a professional. Put yourself in their place, being back there, fourteen, fifteen years old, and having an adult, a professional like a doctor, come in and talk to you. Wouldn't you be more inclined to really listen and possibly be affected or influenced more by someone who was nearer your age? Something you could think about... Could you go to some of the schools?"

"And just do it."

"And just say you did a project several years ago, a n d   y o u ' r e   c o n c e r n e d . And that it also affected you personally in your own life. And maybe you have an idea of some sort of a program where you might be able to go in and just talk to the kids..."

"Yeah, I might think about that."

187

SOMETIMES A STAR...

it must be
a Protestant swallow...

Rev. Peter is a man in his fifties. What I remember most from the first time we met was his wonderful smile and warm manner. He had a boyish quality about him, possibly due to a very generous head of hair he had (mostly white now, with traces of blond throughout). He began speaking immediately, without any prompting.

"I'll give a brief biographical sketch of where I've come from. For the last twenty-one years, Helen, my wife, and our four children, who are all in their late teens and early twenties now, we've been ministering in three parishes in Yorkshire, all fairly working-class parishes. Very poor areas. We'd been in our last place for nearly eleven years. A lot of unemployment, very sort of macho area. A lot of the young people at school knew they wouldn't get jobs when they left, so there's a lot of sort of aggression and cynicism. Very tough area, really. Very hard for teenagers to grow up in. Very hard for teenagers to have any faith in a real sense. Some of them survive by going into a sort of ghetto mentality; others would very much mix in with the local culture. So there were quite a lot of pressures there in some ways, although we enjoyed it.

"We saw quite a lot of growth in the Church, and I would say in the eleven years there, we saw a lot of change and a steady trickle of people coming to faith every year. Mostly adults coming to the faith, rather than teenagers being confirmed. Our last confirmation group ranged in age. There was one teenager; all the rest were over twenty and the oldest was a man of seventy-four. So that's our background. For a couple of years before that, we'd been thinking, the parish could well do with a change, and maybe it was time for a change for us. We'd been praying about a move. And for those couple of years, I'd felt drawn to Ireland in some way. I couldn't put it more strongly than that. I found I was reading a bit more about Ireland, and perhaps the music a little bit. To some extent in England, Irish culture is becoming more popular, y'know. St. Patrick's Day we celebrate in local pubs, and this kind of thing. Usually just transferred to more Guinness!.

"Ever since we got married over twenty years ago, we'd come across the island of Lindisfarne, or Holy Island, in Northumberland. I think Helen and I were just engaged then. We'd been on our way down from some friends in Scotland, and we just stopped one evening at the beach there, just below Lindisfarne. It was just one of those sort of awesome places where we just thought, 'Ah, we must come back here.' And I think almost every year since then, I've taken groups up there. I used to take my curates away and we'd have a retreat there for two or three days. Often in October we'd have a day of silence, and then we'd have a day of frantic activity of planning and preparing stuff and working through things. So Lindisfarne, I would say, became a home almost in one sense. And I know whenever I go back there, immediately I just feel it's one of those 'home' places...

"I'd come across fairly early some of the David Adam books that struck me very deeply, and then of

191

course he eventually became rector of Holy Island. We stayed at the Marygate House, with the community there, when we'd gone out. We'd taken a couple of church groups up from one of our parishes, and they'd always enjoyed it. So, there'd been a link there and some contact with the early Celtic Christians, and I think having read a bit about them in England, about Aidan and people like that, and Cuthbert. There was something of a spark there.

"I was also involved quite a lot with the Anglican renewal ministries. About fifteen years ago now, a man named John Winber came over from the States, and for some reason inside, I felt I was to go to this conference that was on in Sheffield. He used to play with the Righteous Brothers pop group. An incredible character. And a very, very gifted man who had come to faith late in life. He had a wonderful gift of being able to speak about the Holy Spirit and the gifts of the Spirit in a very down-to-earth way. A very humble man, who brought along with him a whole strand of a new sort of dynamic Christian music. He had a great sort of passionate love for God, and yet at the same time a sense of humor. He was down to earth. Somehow I think he just seemed to fit into what many Anglicans in England were looking for at that time, a sort of relevant, modern expression of their faith that was going to somehow fit within the Church of England. I would say that his visits, and the Vineyard—the Ministry of the Vineyard teams and others who came over—had a profound and lasting effect on the Church of England. So that was another strand that had a big impact on me. And through Anglican renewal ministries where they also had a.... I think they called a symposium on Celtic Christianity. It was just beginning to get a little bit fashionable in England then. But it was excellently done, and again it challenged me to read a bit more. You mentioned the other day about this sort of creation thing and about the holistic aspect of faith, about their evangelism, about their emphasis on the Spirit and the gifts of the Spirit. So many strands seem to come together in that, really. And so again, that's perhaps something that was there in the background, as far as Ireland was concerned.

"But I was equally aware that it's easy to have these romantic ideas about the Celtic West and all that, when you've got your nose to the grindstone in a very gritty south Yorkshire industrial parish. But I am aware it was much more than that. And then, as we were looking around, suddenly we noticed in a Church of England newspaper an advertisement for this parish here. We sort of smiled about it a little bit, and we agreed I would send off for details. Now, I didn't know anyone in Ireland, I'd never even been to Ireland. But a few weeks later, I had a phone call from a priest who is now a bishop. We had actually been in college together. As it turned out, he was in Cork. We obviously had known each other a bit in college, but had lost touch since then. He overcame some of my initial problems—would an Englishman even be acceptable over in Southern Ireland, etc. So that encouraged us to take it a step further. I discovered there was a rector nearby who had been a close friend of one of my previous curates. I had actually met him, and I discovered that he was in Cork as well. So there were one or two strange link-ups there. Having thought we knew no one, we suddenly discovered we knew a couple of people. So, we came over for the interview, looked at the house and the church, took one look and thought, oh, no... Everything seemed to be sort of crumbling, really. The house was really damp, with mold.

"The weather was a beautiful week. We were here about five days, and it was a very sunny time, which is unusual for Ireland. We were looking at the parish and having the interview, but for one day we were anxious to travel to the West, and realized how beautiful it was. But that didn't influence the two of us at all, really...

"So, we had the interview with the bishop, and he was more or less assuming from the start that we would take the job. We realized that they hadn't been able to get anyone for about eighteen or twenty months. We began to piece together that obviously it was quite a problem parish, in many senses. So we went back. Helen felt very definitely, 'Oh, we won't be going back,' but somehow I increasingly felt that God was calling us over here. It was a difficult time. We spent a lot of time praying and agonizing over it. I'd felt God saying that I would really have the choice about this, either to come or not to come. But increasingly, things seemed to happen, and meeting people... that just overwhelmingly almost seemed to say that we were to come.

"One particular instance I remember while still in England. We had gone to a conference in Sunderland, and God had seemed very clearly to speak to me from that verse where Paul wasn't sure where to go and he had the vision of the man in Macedonia who said, 'Come over and help us.' Now I've had that several times. I haven't said it to many people, because it sounded a bit arrogant, you know... saying I was going down to

Ireland. Which I thought very much I wasn't! And then I had gone to this conference, and the lady who was speaking there was actually from one of the Vineyard churches, in Vancouver, I think... I'm sorry, from Toronto. They had been praying with various people, and at the end she was just standing there and available, and I went over and just said, 'Look, we've got this very big decision to make. I'd just value some prayer and any insight you feel from God on this.' And she paused for about ten seconds, and said, 'I feel you should go and read the passage in the Book of Acts where Paul had the vision of the man from Macedonia who said "come over and help us".' And so my mouth fell open! There were just two things that happened... So, eventually, we came.

"To be honest, I thought at first, well... they'll be very much the same as England. It's Anglican, they have slightly different accents, but beyond that, it'll be much the same. I think since coming we've been aware of just how totally different they are, culturally and even within the Church of Ireland. How different the feel of so many things is. Now, admittedly, the Church of Ireland parish here obviously was quite run down, and increasingly you'll begin to see some of the reasons for that.

196

Eventually, the bishop put another rector in our house, temporarily, when we'd accepted the job, or just before that. So there were great problems. We found this very difficult. The bishop hadn't obviously found other accommodations for this chap. Originally, he'd been set up to become the rector of two joint parishes in the area. He'd found it so horrendous with some of the relationships here that he wouldn't take the job. So he was remaining in the other town and I was coming here. I was hoping we would be able to work together for maybe a couple of years, to gradually draw things together. And then I knew eventually I would become the rector of the joint parish. But within two months he had managed to get a move and was gone. So I suddenly found myself with this vast geographical area. It would take me, I think, virtually an hour—not quite so much now with the new road open—to drive from one end of the parish to the other. In our last parish, we had eleven thousand people. It would take three or four minutes to drive across. So, that was a contrast. In the church here, a church that would seat five hundred, we had thirty people. On the other end of the parish, a few more... But there were three church buildings there, one of which had to be closed—with an *awful* lot of rankling—

about eighteen months before I had come. There had been a lot of upset because at different times each of those three churches was going to be closed, but it was changed. So there had been a lot of hurt, a lot of wounding over there as well. And so we took on this situation.

"I think for our first year here, we were just amazed at how friendly everyone was... when you'd go into shops or if you'd need any help with anything. People were very, very helpful and very friendly and kind, which was great. I think in the second year, we were aware still of that experience of the first year, but you began to realize how much more was going on under the surface which you only gradually discovered. At times great pain, great anguish, a lot of covering up of past hurts, a lot of past history in the Church of Ireland, of fallings out and this kind of thing. I think by the third year we began to sort of integrate those things.

"The Church of Ireland, particularly in this town, there were two churches here because the British Navy was here in the past. One was closed in the 1960s, which supposedly was 'our' church, according to a number of people who don't come anymore. This is the one some of the Navy came to when the British were here. The one nearby, as some still refer to as the 'snobs' church, was where the officers went. And it was the one 'over there' that was kept open. I think probably because physically it was in slightly better shape, although others would have argued on that. So, buildings in the Church of Ireland have always been of major significance (I think this is the reason historically). Whereas in England they'd be much more certainly in the cities and towns, places of worship and ministry and everything else and would be adapted when this was necessary. Keeping the buildings is very important, I s'pose, for some individuals. There's past history there, the Church of Ireland being a minority. The important thing is to keep your identity. There's a very strong tribal feeling. There'd be a lot of people who call themselves atheists or agnostics who would still very much be Church of Ireland. You have to do a census, you see, of who's Church of Ireland, how many families you've got. And this has to include those who don't normally attend. But when I asked the question, 'Well, should people be on the list who would describe themselves as atheists or agnostics?' 'Certainly,' I was told by some people, 'if they're Church of Ireland, they're Church of Ireland.' So, whether they're agnostics or atheists didn't really matter. The important thing is the identity or the tribal thing, really.

"So, buildings are very important, keeping up appearances, 'maintaining your presence,' again, is a phrase that's used. A letter that was sent to the Bishop a few years before we came, that's in the file, was talking about this town as being the 'flagship of the Church of Ireland.' So, there you've got tiny numbers, a building which has not been decorated—there's no interest to do anything with it, or doesn't seem to be—where you can't get anyone to maintain the grounds. They say they're too old and just don't want to be involved in it. But the building has to remain, and they'll do whatever they can to get money, to manipulate or maneuver, to keep the roof on the place, to preserve the identity.

"I was talking with someone... With the rectory in a terrible state and obviously a new parish, the sensible thing was to have a rectory more geographically halfway between the two parishes. There was actually a house, they purchased the site, and we were told at the interview it would be the new house within six months. Not that we're looking for a new house, but the one we're in, as I say, the damp and the other things were terrible. But it was a very big house, with big grounds. It didn't matter whether the grounds hadn't been maintained by previous rectors. The important thing was that it suited the

200

style in which they expected their rectors to be seen in, even though you had a salary with which you couldn't maintain it. It felt sometimes like the Pharisees, where Jesus says they put heavy burdens on people. That might sound unkind, but it felt like that sometimes, because you didn't own the house. There were two people who were wardens who were responsible for maintaining it. Some work was done on it. But the way the system worked, it was always done through a particular architect or a particular builder, and although outwardly you thought things were being done fairly, it always worked in the same way, that the same people were used and the work was often botched. For instance, we have water pouring down the inside of our bedroom. The builder was called in to deal with this and he got a piece of old wood—not even new wood—he got from somewhere. Measured it so it fitted in between the windows where the water was coming down, and he screwed it onto the wall without any paint or anything over it. That was the solution to this water running down. So there were a number of memories like this.

"And so, as some saw it here in town, they 'lost their rectory.' This was a major defeat. One of the men, a man who's very much been in control in the town, said,

'That's the end of the Church of Ireland in this town.' The church was still open, services held regularly, still a rector covering the area. But they saw the fact that the rectory was going out of town as the end of the Church of Ireland here. So, it's a very different way of looking at things, there seems very little—from my perspective, anyway, and I don't want to judge or condemn people— very little or no apparent spiritual interest at all here. When we've had fellowship groups or suggest prayer or anything like that, no one will come, really, from town. In the parish as a whole, we'd get perhaps five or six people who would come and show some interest. I was told when I arrived here, it was the first week. I think it was the person who is now bishop. He said, 'Coming to the Church of Ireland, particularly in this town, is like joining a tennis club where no one mentions the word 'tennis.' And I eventually realized what he meant by this…

"When we had the first 'Week of Prayer for Christian Unity' service, my immediate concern was obviously to make links in the community here, with the Christian Fellowship and with the Catholic community (when we were in England, we were accustomed to working with different denominations.) We met regularly for prayer with the Catholic priest, the Methodist minister and a few other ministers. We all got on very well. I found them to be very open and welcoming here. I never know what goes on under the surface too much, but they've always been very open. We've done a number of joint things together, and that's been great. They traditionally had a 'week of prayer' service together, and this particular year—I think it was the first year I was here— the service suggested that there be someone from each of the faith communities who could share a little bit about their experience of faith, or about their faith journey, a sort of testimony thing, or whatever you'd like to refer to it as. Someone came from the Catholic community and someone came from the Christian Fellowship. But when I asked for someone who'd volunteer from our congregation... nothing. So I brought it to the vestry, the select vestry—sort of a committee, a church council with lay people who help to run the parish. So, I brought it there and said, 'Look, we've got this service coming, we need someone.' I sort of tried to just shame them a little bit. 'This is an ecumenical service. We need someone from the Church of Ireland here to share in this and to be involved.' So they delegated one person who had not been at the meeting and said, 'Oh, he'll do it, he's good at public speaking.' This was one of our gentleman farmers who has actually been very involved in the community, but very much staunchly Church of Ireland. So, I asked him. He was very, very hesitant, but in the end he agreed, for keeping up our end of things and not losing face. Losing face is a very serious thing, within the Church of Ireland particularly. The service came round, and we had two very warm and personal sharings by the two other folks. When it came to the Church of Ireland, the man who was contributing simply said, 'Well, here in the Church of Ireland, we don't talk about our faith; we believe it's a private matter. We believe that it all depends on those two commandments of Jesus, to love God and to love your neighbor, and the second is the most important.' And then he sat down. That was it, really! Everyone, I think, was a little bit stunned by it. But in some ways, I think that summed up what many people would say or feel within the Church of Ireland...

"So, a lot of all this has to do with buildings and keeping buildings open. And I s'pose I had to discover very rapidly there are obviously totally different agendas going on. The church here is very much controlled by one man. Has been in the past. They've come under him and allowed him to do the work and any decisions that had to be made. He's a very able man on finances and buildings. Well, not so much on buildings, but as getting things done. There's been an awful lot of, I could honestly say, of what I see as control and manipulation in the past. And people have opted out. Some of the younger folks who were involved in the Church Council with their own ideas just found that they were never listened to. Decisions wouldn't be voted on. It was done by consensus, as they said. So this ruling group would say, 'Right, this is how we're doing it, and that's it.' Previous rectors, as well, have opted out and gone because of not being able to cope with this. They tended to have younger men here, being a small parish. The last chap stayed for just eighteen months and, as I said, there was a gap of, say, eighteen to twenty-one months in between...

"So, that's been the situation, really. It's been quite an eye-opener. By now, at least they've had two parishes that are joined. I've had the difficult job of trying to bring them together, and to try and see that both ends are treated fairly. All of them to some extent, but particularly here. There seems to be this need to just look after their own end and keep their own end up. There've almost been battles about getting money for *their* church, not for anyone else's, and for keeping this open and not that. So everything is seen in these terms. And very, very little apparent spiritual interest, or openness to visitors.

"Now I do feel, y'know, the Church of Ireland at its best, or the Anglican Church at its best, has got a lot to give. Many, many Catholics wanted to learn the Scriptures. Sales of Bibles have shot up in recent years, and I found when we've done joint Alpha groups— we've done a lot of joint groups at both ends of the parish—it'll be the Catholics who have come, and will hang on every word, really, which is frightening as you're speaking and sharing about the Bible. They want more and more and more. But we just can't seem to get any, or very few, of the Church of Ireland folks who would come along to that. So I find I'm a bit schizo-phrenic, really! Now probably proportionately, out of the large numbers who'd attend the Catholic Church, these are only a small number. But there's a great hunger among a lot of them, just to talk about the faith, to ask questions, to study the Scriptures so that they can find out more for themselves about it. So that's been the one heartening thing. I know when we started the Alpha group, there was a lovely Catholic couple who'd been working with us here, a lay couple. They'd been tremendous. And we also had the daughter of the pastor of the Christian Fellowship here. She was playing the guitar and leading the worship. So it was very much an ecumenical or a united group that was helping with these Alphas. The first time we met, we had sixty people who came. Ninety-five percent of those were Catholics. Fifty of them stayed for the eleven weeks."

"Could you say some more about Alpha, and possibly something about your upbringing?"

"Alpha started over in England. We found, with a lot of people in England, there would be an inner longing for something, a searching there among many people. In my background, I never went to church as a child or never went to Sunday school or anything else. I was baptized in the Anglican Church, but my parents never went. Most of my generation would have gone to Sunday school, although I never did. I was confirmed at fifteen through school, simply because the chaplain came in and persuaded the headmaster to let us off from some of the homework if we went to confirmation classes. I can't remember anything about it, really, except we were told how to genuflect and various things... not to wear Brylcreem when the Bishop came or he would get his hands greasy. There was nothing I remember about faith, or about relating it to us, really. What we'd used to do was to say to the rather elderly chap, 'Please, sir, what does circumcision mean?' and things like that. And he would go bright red and say, 'Shut up, boy' and that would be it. So that's my memory of confirmation. After that, I felt I ought to go to church a bit, as I was now somewhat religious. I went to our local church where I lived in Nottingham. I think I went three times. No one spoke to me. It was a very dark, gloomy place, I remember... And one of my memories is that the vicar there was a very heavy smoker, because when he gave you Communion, his hands were all stained with nicotine. That wouldn't bother me much now, but at fifteen I used to think, well, that's a bit funny. After three or four times, I thought, 'I'm not interested in religion anymore.'

"It wasn't for another four years... I went to college and I met some folks who were 'Christians.' They just seemed so full of life and everything. And at that time I was beginning, I think, to search myself... for something. I remember thinking, OK, you go to university, you work, you get a job, you get married, have kids grow up, and die. There's got to be more to life than this! And other things like that I was beginning to think about. But those folks I met when I went to college, it was their sort of love of life and the joy they seemed to have, and the way they seemed to have life together much more than me. That, I think, initially attracted me and got me thinking. I was aware there was a whole area of life that I had never really even thought about before. And I think there a lot of people in England who would be like that, not going to church. It would be hard to make that transition from being a total outsider, as I was, to actually go into a strange place where you had to stand up, sit down, and do peculiar things. And sing, which of course you'd never be used to doing, except in a pub. So, we found that we tried to have easy ways for people to come in, they would come. We'd often have meetings or groups in pubs, where you'd meet people there, or men's groups, where you could invite people perhaps you'd have contact with, to come along to a group. Informal, where you got refreshments, where you could just sit down, where they could ask questions, where there was no pressure on them. And they could explore perhaps in a relevant and modern way something of what faith meant. I think the Alpha course seemed to just catch that. And now, of course, it's spread throughout the whole world.

"I believe there are over a million people in England now who have actually done Alpha courses. It's a basic introduction to the Christian faith. It's done with quite a bit of humor. There's a talk, there's always some food or a meal or refreshments. It's worked well in London, where a lot of the Yuppies come in for a meal after work. And there's always time for discussion questions. There's a weekend away where there's teaching on the Holy Spirit and there's prayer for people to receive the Holy Spirit. In one sense, it's quite, if you like, charismatic. But not in a sort of over-the-top way. But an opportunity   for people actually to be open to God, to experience God, and for many of the people, that has been the time where things have just turned around for them. We found that in many ways here, there was quite a lot of questioning, as I said. It was fascinating, talking particularly to some of the older Catholic folks. To begin with, they felt very threatened by the whole process of asking or being able to ask questions or having ideas or opinions of their own. Because for many in that generation, they'd been brought up in such a way that this was a sign of a lack of faith, if you asked questions or had

210

your own ideas. You had to accept, and that was it. But gradually, as they got used to this, many of them found that they were able to look at issues and to ask questions, and understand things which they had never been able to do before. I remember the very first question we had in the group, and this for me coming over as an Anglican to Ireland. The first question that came up in our group from a Catholic lady was, 'Tell me, Rector, what's happened to Limbo?' Now, I didn't know whether she was talking about limbo-dancing from the West Indies" (*some laughter*) "but I very quickly realized that obviously she was talking about, y'know," (*his voice softening*) "what happened to babies who died who hadn't been baptized. Obviously, this had been something that had been taught very much in Ireland, but seemed to have faded out in recent years. She was very concerned that it hadn't been mentioned much in the Catholic Church. So those were a few initial things..."

(After quite a long pause, Peter continued.)

"I found that, although I s'pose I came over with an interest in the English Celtic saints, particularly from Northumberland, I don't think I was aware 'til I came

211

here that St. Patrick was actually an Englishman, or maybe a Welshman. My wife came from Cumbria, and there's a strong tradition that Patrick actually came from the Lake District, from the Cumbria area... I don't know. But anyway, that was interesting. I read his Confessions, and the more definite things about Patrick, and again there was quite a lot of inspiration in that, really. But the same Celtic strands were there obviously with the others, the distances they traveled, and I think just their relating to ordinary people. And I s'pose for historic reasons, the Church of Ireland has often seemed to be and still has this faint whiff of ascendancy about it.

"I think I mentioned to you that story about the swallow that got into church a few weeks ago. I was just packing my bags, getting ready to go on to the next service, and there were a few parishioners still left in the church. I don't think they knew I was there. Obviously, a swallow had flown into the church at the end of the service, and one of our farmers said, 'Oh, it must be a Protestant swallow.' And I heard this older lady, who's very, very nice—very Church of Ireland—just say, jokingly I'm sure, 'Oh, it must be a better kind of swallow.' And in some ways that epitomizes that although the numbers may be very small, we're still somehow... just,

212

perhaps, a little better. And yet within the Church of Ireland, I s'pose much more than what I'm used to, from England, you've got a very broad cross-section of backgrounds. There are quite a few folks who would be called West Brits over here. When I first came, I made the mistake early on of thinking they were English. They sounded, well, as they say in Yorkshire, very 'posh.' You'd hear about these people who lived down in Surrey and places like this down south, but we never really met them in Yorkshire where we were. So they'd sound like very well-educated southerners from England, from certain parts of the South. So I said, 'Oh, you're from England, are you,' and they'd say, 'Goodness, gracious me... no, we're from Dublin.' But many of them came from wealthy families who had been educated in Anglican and British schools. There are quite a lot of those kinds of families around, who would very much see themselves as being rather 'better' than others. They would frown on me mixing with 'them,' and even down here in the south of Ireland, there's a lot of hidden sectarianism, I find, just in attitudes. They would still say, 'Y'know, we're having the renovations done on our new rectory,' and I was told, 'Try to get Sam. He's one of *ours*, you know...' So there's still a lot of this kind of thing going on underneath. Certainly forty years ago in Cork, they would know who the Protestant businesses were, and who the Catholic ones were. Many of them would be on Patrick Street, and of course you would patronize those that were 'ours,' and avoided 'them.' But this was, um, y'know, swept under the carpet a little. But this is still perpetrated underneath rather strongly by quite a few people."

"So you think this kind of attitude continues under the surface?"

"Oh, under the surface, I would say that it is still quite strong. And certainly I've heard comments like, 'He's meant to be a rector of the Church of Ireland. I don't know what he's doing mixing with them...' *Them* all the time. So it's still seen that the rector should be 'mixing with ours.' They expect you to be seen in the community. I find it fascinating here that you get invited to bless this and to bless that, all kinds of community things. So you have quite a public face in one sense. As someone said we have what, two percent... five percent the very most, in some areas of the population. But fifty percent of the appearances! So, if they invite a Catholic priest to come and bless a new facility, they would also invite the Church of Ireland rector, and then to do the prayer of blessing. So it's very nice to get invited to these things, y'know. Lovely meals, and you meet some fascinating people. Whereas over in England, I'd never really meet the local MP. Over here, you meet the TV people, the ministers that come to all these local things. I've met the President... all the politicians, and different people, just in a few years. I'm chaplain to the naval base here, chaplain to the port of call, chaplain to the prison nearby. Sounds wonderful! But of course there are very few Church of Ireland people there, so you get invited to the ceremonial occasions and the dinners sometimes. But there's very little actually to do in that sense. So much of the time in the Church of Ireland, they would still expect you to spend most of your time visiting. They wouldn't see it in terms of them doing any of these things, or it being a shared sort of thing. The rector visits 'ours.' And certainly, up to twenty years ago and probably after that, it would still be seen as a very, very big mistake to actually go visit one of 'theirs.' Y'know, you have to just visit 'ours.' I was told the other week that if you'd got the wrong address and went to see one of theirs, that would be seen as very unfortunate.

"So, there's no concept of reaching out to others. Many people would be agnostic now within the community; you have to be very careful you're not seen to be proselytizing. So there's no concept, really, of people being , well to use the phrase 'converted to Christ.' You are either converting to 'them,' to being a Catholic, or they're converting to us and becoming the Church of Ireland. Which I find strange. And again, words mean different things. In England, whatever their denomination or background, people would have referred to themselves generally as Christians. Over here, I've met people who said, 'Oh, no, I'm not a Christian... I'm a Catholic.' I've met people who said, 'I'm definitely not a Christian. I'm Church of Ireland.' The word 'Christian' is often used to signify anyone else, and you're often referred to as the 'born-agains,' and they're linked in with the sects, like the Jehovah's Witnesses and the Scientologists. Y'see, you have to be very careful. So, among many people, the lines are carefully drawn. Obviously, a lot of young people are exploring all kinds of weird and wonderful ideas and religions and different things. There's almost a great paranoia of sects, even though the Pentecostals now would have three hundred and fifty million world-wide. They would still be seen

216

here as, 'oh, you know, they're the 'born-agains,' and everyone seems almost to be lumped together with the 'born-agains.' Methodists might just about be OK, but anyone else is really lumped with these others, and classed as a sect.

"So, it's a very strangely divided system. You're either Catholic or you're Protestant. Protestant would usually mean Church of' Ireland, with maybe a few Methodists. That's where the lines are drawn. There are no non-Christians, in many people's eyes. You're either one or the other, and it depends what you're baptized into. And what you are baptized into, in many people's eyes, seems to be the thing that decides for life what you are. Now, those lines are breaking down a bit; obviously we have a number of couples who'd be from mixed marriages. Maybe there's a Catholic wife or a Catholic husband. And I am sure that would be true in the Catholic Church as well. But still an awful lot of bitterness in the Church of Ireland with the thing about mixed marriages. For insistence with the Catholic Church, in a mixed marriage, the children have to be baptized as Catholics and brought up as Catholics. There's the film, 'A Love Divided,' which you must see if you get the chance. About what happened; I think it was in County Wexford,

217

in the 1950's. There was a mixed marriage, and the Church of Ireland wife wanted the children to go to the Church of Ireland school, and there was a boycott of all Protestant businesses. It's a fascinating film, very beautifully made. But that is in very recent memory, in people's minds.

"There's a little bitterness from the past, I think, among Church of Ireland people as numbers go down. 'Oh, they stole our children from us.' They would often have these Protestant dances. They still do in the West. These are basically sort of marriage bureaus, where you'd have these specifically Protestant events. There would be an opportunity for the young people to meet other Protestant young people, so they could find marriage partners. If it was a mixed marriage, there was this terror; there was this decree from the Catholic Church. They had to sign away their children. So there's a lot of bitterness still there... 'they stole our children from us.' Now, although that decree is being revoked, I think officially, there are still some Catholic priests who are trying to enforce it. There's been a lot of hurt among young couples in mixed marriages over it, I think, in the past.

"So that was one negative, I s'pose, from the Church of Ireland or the Protestant side. I s'pose from the

218

Catholic side, as well, there's been an awful lot of terrible pain from the history and the way the British and the ruling classes controlled them and refused to allow them to practice their faith. So those wounds are still very deep... and understandable. And I s'pose we still have these West Brit Church of Ireland families who speak in a very superior manner, and their attitudes. They come over with a terrible arrogance sometimes. This feeling of the 'ascendancy,' I suspect, can still create a lot of pain. And ill feeling that many will become Catholics. I mentioned earlier a man who very much has controlled the Church of Ireland locally. There are people in the town, Catholics, who've worked under him in different situations and have found this attitude very hard to cope with. There's nothing you can do about it, his upbringing and the way he's been used to treating people. But the feeling that others get from it is not good..." *(Sigh.)* "Right... I've run out of steam!" *(A strong laugh.)*

(After a few minutes' break, we continued. I asked Peter if he could say some more about his own experience, his feelings, and what he saw for the future.)

"I think, looking back, it's been very stimulating;

219

it's been very challenging. I'm in my fifties now. There are times that it's been almost breathtakingly different and hard to adjust to. But it's been exhilarating, as I said, at the same time. It's been very eye-opening and I've been very humbled really to just be aware, and saddened, how little I knew of the real Irish history. You learn history through your own tinted specs, through your own culture, really. So that's been a very humbling thing. It's been great, I think, to learn about a very different culture and to experience a lot of interesting things, and so many wonderful people through it all. But I would still say we feel very much strangers in a strange land, because we have no roots here. I think for many Irish people, roots are important. If you meet someone in the Church of Ireland, the first question they ask is 'Where are you from?' or 'Do you know so-and-so?' Once they've placed you, you're OK. But we have no relatives here, so they're often lost as how to fit you into their scheme of things—which sometimes can be difficult. You feel quite isolated. There's not as much warmth in the churches generally over here as we've been used to in England, in Yorkshire. But particularly in our parish, the farmers have been very warm. I know this one farmer's wife who's always been very friendly, and

220

I think I had been here about a year and she always seemed so pleased to see me. She would start patting me on my bottom when we were saying good-bye at church on Sunday morning. So I realized that I was accepted!" *(Laughter.)* "Now there's nothing untoward about that. She was just being friendly, just seemed so pleased to see you. And she always gives me a hug now and a kiss, just in a natural way, which we were used to with many of our folks in Yorkshire. There's a lot of warmth there with them. And there are a number of, I'd say, ordinary people in the parish who would be delightful, some really lovely people. But what a contrast between them, and some of the more wealthy ones. Now maybe it's just the culture; I'm not from that background. For many of them, obviously from perhaps their public school backgrounds, they find it very difficult to relate to others. They're very fearful about expressing any emotions. We have the 'peace' now within the Anglican Church, of sharing that. They would be terrified by that sort of thing.

"So you've got all of these different strands flowing through the Church of Ireland, and difficult to bring them together. But I think among some, what we would call perhaps the West Brit families, there's a lot of fear, as well, because they've lost a lot of their position in society. They've still got their money around, I s'pose, but maybe a lot of their position in society is gone now. And power. Often when we have a parish lunch together every year on the anniversary when the parish joined up, we would generally get a good turn-out for that, a good time. Interestingly, even though there'd been separation among the parish, and squabbling between them, when we have these big tables of ten people, the West Brit ones would always sit together. It was fascinating; on one such occasion, there was one spare place at their table. There was a couple from a town nearby that came in late. There were just two places left, one of which was at this table. So the wife sat at this table, and it was very much socially a completely different table of people. One of them was overheard by someone else saying, 'Well, it was a very nice meal, but, uh, it was a shame that we had to have *her* coming and sitting with us.' I was just, well... if I had heard that about myself, I would have been so angry. But, sadly, there's that kind of attitude, still there underneath, with some of them. So it's difficult to draw all this mixture of people together, especially when there seems outwardly so little real faith there. Which, I believe, is the only ingredient that will actually overcome these differences and cement them together in Christ.

"Now, the future... Well, I s'pose I see the Church of Ireland dying, to be honest, at the moment. But it's a death with a resurrection. I think I said something on this a bit earlier. We have an awful lot to offer. There's our knowledge of the Scriptures and our willingness to share those, which many Catholics are searching for and looking for. I really believe our liturgy has a great deal to offer. I meet a lot of people who perhaps don't go to Mass regularly now, who would see themselves as believers still, but not within, really, the Catholic system. Many of them would be put off with the moving statues—very cynical about the moving statues and all this kind of thing—and yet they are looking for some richness and some reality that would somehow draw it together. And I believe a lot of our Celtic roots, which I would say are common to all these Catholics, Church of Ireland, whatever. All these strands... if somehow we can get back to that, but in a new way, and learn from that, and the holistic sense that the Celtic Christians seemed to have. I think there is a very real way forward there. Our bishop said to me the other day that young people are no longer interested today in denominations. And I don't think they are. They're interested in people. I would say 'amen' to that! Y'know, God just delights in people! And somehow if we can move away from this preoccupation with buildings and keeping buildings open... There is a rich vein of Celtic music—why do the pubs have to have it all, and none of it or very little of it in worship? There are some who are writing modern Celtic Christian music, which, I believe, would draw us all together. And I think many of the Catholics are now looking for more worship and singing, which they have not always had in their own communities. So I think if we could somehow within the Church of Ireland search out and create some modern strands. We're still very much stuck with all the old and the traditional (although there are some wonderful things there). I think there's a very rich strand there of music which has a depth to it and a breadth to it, but if it was brought into Christian worship it would be a tremendously enriching thing, and would be valued here in the culture of Ireland. And, I am sure, would bless many other people, too.

"Getting back to what the Church of Ireland has to offer. I think there's the worship, I think there's the Biblical roots to it, and hopefully, as well, in its best sense, the Anglican Church should be open. There's an openness there to all, really. Now I know you can be so open that everything drops out at both ends. Y'know, in Ireland there has been this closed-ness, really, within all the churches. That's breaking down now. But I think if we can create a church in Ireland which is post-denominational, which is open to everyone... God seems to have been saying lately that he's drawing in the farmers and the fugitives to Ireland somehow... open to all these people. There are many, many ordinary people in Ireland who are struggling with life.

"In our joint mid-week group recently—I was in a group with one Church of Ireland lady and two Catholics—I asked them to share with one another just two things they would like others to pray for in that group. And it turned out every one of the people in that group, who outwardly seemed fine, had someone who was seriously mentally ill within their family. Two of them had mentally sick husbands, and for the first time, almost, they were able to talk about that as tears came

down their faces. Another one had a mentally handi-
capped son of twenty-nine, and the pain of looking after
him and dealing with that. And I was just amazed that
here in this group, everything seemed fine. But as we
shared, out of those three people in my group, each of
them was feeling terrible pain that they were able just to
share and to speak about.

"In the past, the Catholic Church has obviously had
such vast numbers. When we first arrived, we thought
there was a football match on, the Sunday when we first
came over for our interview. There were all these
crowds of people! And we suddenly realized they were
coming out of church. And we just couldn't believe it...
So the numbers have been there, and still are to some
extent, although they're going down rapidly. But within
that, many Catholics will say, 'But we never see the
priest' or 'He never comes to the door afterwards', or 'He
doesn't know who we are.' So there's an opportunity
somehow in having cell groups or home groups where
people can actually relate in a real way and share their
needs, as well as their joys. I think, again, perhaps that's
something which we could offer. I've heard an awful lot
of Catholics say, 'Oh, you're fortunate in your church...

there's a lovely family atmosphere there.' I would say that in reality there's a very cold atmosphere there often, and a very rigid atmosphere. But they sense because we've got small numbers, somehow it's going to be more intimate. There are some churches where it is within the Church of Ireland, but it isn't always present. I think that's something, again, which perhaps we can share and benefit from together.

"On my first Sunday, I really thought I had done something wrong, or I was dressed wrong. I thought it was my accent, because when I came to say the service, everyone just sort of... seemed so... serious, and um, had sort of grim expressions on their faces. And I thought, 'Oh, dear, what is it?' It was like that all the way through the service, even in the sermon. I told what I thought was a funny story and there was no sign of any movement or smiles or anything. I thought, well... maybe it's my sense of humor or something. And then over coffee, everyone seemed to be chatting normally, and I began to realize that this was, somehow, church on Sunday morning. Now, they've loosened up a little bit since then. But I was just stunned by that... So there's a rigidness there often that has been associated with the Church of Ireland.

"I want to just tell one other quick story. We were invited to a lunch, a family celebration to celebrate one hundred years of the family coming here, a farming family, fairly wealthy. Others would describe them as gentlemen farmers. So we came to this lunch, and relatives had come from different parts of the world, actually. We had the lunch, a very nice meal. And afterwards one of their relatives, who came from an area which is much more of a sort of Protestant area, was providing the after-dinner entertainment. And this entertainment consisted of reading through the minutes of the select vestry meetings of that parish in the early 1900s, and reading through the disputes that had taken place between the Earl of Bandon and the great-grandfather of this man who is now here. And about the terrible fall-outs and the quarrels and squabbles they'd had over the minutiae of church procedures and this kind of thing. My wife and I just sort of sat there, and I think if we had just heard this being read to us, we would have almost wept with sadness at what had been happening in this church. Personalities just tearing each other apart. But I think the most fearsome thing or frightening for us was that this was, in a sense, provided as after-dinner entertainment. And there was quite a degree of laughing. It would have been very amusing if it hadn't been so tragic, in a sense. This was a family defending their rights, almost, against this other branch of the Church of Ireland. So, there have been experiences like that which have been culturally just absolute eye-openers..."

"Phew! Thanks so much, Peter."

SOMETIMES A STAR...

and then things changed...

Kathleen and Leo are a couple in their sixties, with grown children and grandchildren.
Kathleen was the first to tell her story.

"I was born in the 1940s to a family of four. We were a Catholic family, and we had a very happy home. My mother and father would take us to church, to Mass, to Benediction in the evening, and we would have a Rosary in our house. We were very aware of the church, and the priests, and the religious at the time. We held them in great respect. I went to a Catholic school run by 'Mercy' Sisters. Had a good education, grew up, then left school and went to work, still living at home and

231

enjoying a very happy life. After four or five years, I got married to my husband, in 1964. We had our children quickly and settled down to rear our family. We also wanted to teach them the faith, the Mass-going and praying, and the value of prayer in their life. We gave most of our lives to them."

"What are some of those memories from your childhood?"

"Just gathered together at home, doing our homework, just being a family, being together. Listening to the radio was a great hobby of ours. We listened to 'Question Time,' and Irish dance music, and the news. We were all there together, six of us, mother and father and four children. And then there were the days when we went out together, for a trip on the bus, to the seaside, and a picnic. We would visit our relations, our friends. What I remember mostly about our Sunday mornings was that my father, after Mass, would gather us together, the four of us—while my mother prepared the dinner, cooked it—we would go to the local cemetery to visit his mother's grave, my grandmother. We would do that nearly every Sunday morning, and continue on to our first cousin's house, have a half-an-hour chat, returning *on the dot* of 1 o'clock for our dinner, as it would be ready and be put on the table at one o'clock." *(Pausing, voice dropping.)* "...wonderful... Playing, having games, family... and playing with my sisters and my brothers. And y'know, having a bit of a row with them too! But we always made up afterwards. They were happy memories, really."

"And then after you were married, and you raised your family. I am guessing it was very similar to your own upbringing."

"Very much the same. We would have been a family unit. Leo and I would have worked together to bring up our children and support them and take them to school. And all this kind of work together, the rearing of them, we would have created the same atmosphere as we had in our own homes. And certainly one of the most important things in our life was our religion, and passing that on, giving good example, taking them to Mass and to the church. And getting them involved in prayers, taking them to the Sacraments, making sure it was received properly and taken properly, until they got big enough to

233

make their own minds up... And then things changed..."
(*A soft chuckle.*)

"I suppose I would say, it was in the mid-'70s, early 1980s. Society changed, really. Parents started to leave their families at home with babysitters while they went out enjoying themselves, and they went away on weekends. And as the children grew up then, they followed suit. I feel that's when Ireland began to change, really... for the worse. Family life began to dwindle. I feel that's a terrible pity, and that's the truth. It was a happy time when the family was together, and lived as a family, and they were concerned about one another. But nowadays that seems to have gone... due to, well, everybody being better off, and coming up in the world. Money is more plentiful than it was thirty years ago, forty years ago."

"What do you find life-giving in your life, what sustains you?"

"What sustains me is my relationship with God. No matter what goes wrong, and there have been many ups and downs—more downs than ups—I'm always aware that the Lord is there with me, and all I have to do is turn to Him, and He helps me. That really is what sustains me and keeps me going. And life, no matter what happens, it never overpowers me because I know I have this faith, I have this in my heart. It gives me great hope and great reason for living and just keeping going."

(I thanked Kathleen, and then Leo shared some of his story.)

"I was born in 1936, the youngest of a family of ten. My father died when I was two years old, so my mother had a fairly tough job bringing us up. But she never lost her faith; she always had a great trust in God. She always made sure that we went to Mass every Sunday. From the age of seven, when I made my first Holy Communion, I couldn't wait to be an altar boy, to be serving on the altar. And I served as an altar boy from the age of seven 'til I was twenty-one. So I always had a close connection with the Church. I always had a great attraction to religion. All of my brothers and sisters left home at an early age, because in those days in Ireland, you had no option but to get the boat to England—or further afield, if you could afford to. But England was the gateway for

235

the Irish people to earn their living, so all my brothers and sisters had gone. I was just left at home with one sister, and as I said, my mother had quite a struggle bringing us up. But she always had great trust in God. So I went to work, then, in a garage. I was happy enough bringing home the small wages we got in those days. But I felt the Lord was calling me into a deeper relationship with Him, so I decided to try my vocation in the Cistercian Monastery of Mount Mallory. I stayed there for six months, but I didn't feel it was the life for me. I felt it was too inactive an order and I wanted something more dynamic. I could work in the missions, maybe. So I came home for a while, and then I went to the Jesuits in England. I was there for two and half years, but I finally accepted that the Lord had something else in mind for me to do; it wasn't in His service.

"So I came back and resumed my life working in the garage, and there I met and fell in love with my wife, Kathleen. After a few years going together, we got married and a year after we were married, the Lord blessed us with our first child, and we carried on the tradition of bringing up our children that we had inherited from our respective parents. As each child came along, we made sure the child was baptized. In those days, immediately...

It was a funny custom in those days in the Catholic Church; the mother was still in hospital while the child was taken from her and baptized. The mother wasn't at the baptism at all. That has changed now, thank God! So she never saw the baptism of our first three children. 'Twas only later that the liturgy changed when the child was baptized, preferably on Easter... Holy Saturday night.

"As I said, we did our best not to drag the children along by the hair on their head into religion, but to encourage 'em, pass on the faith that we got. And we made sure we said the Rosary regularly in our house and we brought them to different ceremonies.

"Later on in our life, then, we got introduced to the charismatic renewal, and that was the turning point in our life, really. We didn't know the Holy Spirit up to that stage. It was referred to in the Catholic Church as a ghost. And you don't talk about ghosts! One of our daughters, when she started going to secretarial school, she came home and told my wife one evening about this meeting they were having where people clapped their hands and held their hands up in the air and prayed in these weird tongues. My wife said she'd go along to see what was happening. She thought it was the funniest

237

thing ever. The first meeting, she broke her heart laughing at all these people talking in tongues and praising God out loud. We were always taught to keep our religion very quiet. In those days, when we were growing up, we had the priest saying Mass with his back turned to us, speaking in a language we didn't understand unless we learned Latin. And in those days growing up, the priest was revered, as if he was a king. The priest was the pillar of the society. He couldn't do anything wrong. Then we saw, in the charismatic movement, we saw a greater freedom of expression, and people testifying what God did in their lives. And that transformed us, and gave us a new outlook on life.

"We had the usual problems going through life, raising a family, and all the teenagers' problems. But we felt our religion sustained us, and our belief in God. Many times we wouldn't have persevered if we hadn't had that deep faith. And as the 1980's came along, and coming up to the '90s, life became a bit more affluent for people. A lot of American and Japanese firms moved into Ireland, and they created a bigger economic boom. People began turning away from God, and putting their trust in money. Then we had the first scandal in our church. Because of our upbringing, we never thought of a priest or a nun as being human, that they have some special, God-given gift. We never thought they could commit sins of the flesh. And our first shock was when Bishop Casey, it was announced that he had fathered a child. And my greatest hurt in hearing that was the vision of him standing up beside Pope John Paul in Galway, when Pope John Paul visited Ireland in 1979, and Bishop Casey was standing up beside him shoutin' and roaring that he was the bishop of Galway... knowing all the time that he was living a falsehood and had fathered a child. When that broke in the Catholic Church, it was the start, I'm afraid, of the downfall.

"Then along came different stories of priests who had abused children. And the orphanages. I was born and reared beside an orphanage, and we looked up to those people as fantastic individuals who took in children and cared for them. But it emerged, with all the scandals, that they had abused children and treated them in horrible ways. And slowly but surely, like the Berlin Wall, the Catholic Church started crumbling before our eyes. It wasn't the pillar of society we thought it was. And as a result, I am convinced that an awful lot of young people, when they saw their leaders and what they were capable of doing, and they realized... Young people turned away from the Church. And a lot of not-so-young people, too. We have this state today where there's no respect at all for the Church, and there are very few young people going to Mass. We have this state where an awful lot of people are not getting married now at all. They think it's just normal to live together and have children out of wedlock. So, at the moment I am very depressed, and don't see any great future for the Church. I have a great priest, a priest who says there's going to be a big outpouring of the Holy Spirit in the new millennium. I sincerely hope he's right because I certainly can't see any great hope. There's a lot of laxity amongst the priests, and they're rushing around and they're too busy to listen to you or carry out their normal duties. So I'm just hoping that in the new millennium, we'll definitely have an outpouring of the Holy Spirit because we need something. Because the Church and society are in disarray at the moment. So, they're my thoughts. That enough?" *(Short laugh.)*

"What sustains you?"

"My faith. I have a deep faith. I remember, when I left the Jesuits, the priest called me in to have a chat with

240

me, and he said, 'You have a very deep faith; you'll never lose your faith.' So that's what sustains me, apart from all the things I read. The down things I read about the Church, I still maintain there's a loving God there who's prepared to look after us, and that we are being led by a very good Pope, and that we should listen to his teachings, and try to live our life as good as we can... and not put our trust in material things." *(He smiled.)* "All right?"

"Thank you."

"Welcome."

SOMETIMES A STAR...

the bride at every wedding and the corpse at every wake...

A Dialogue with Liam Lawton

Liam and I met at a restaurant on the outskirts of Limerick. Following a lovely lunch, he suggested we go out to his car in the parking lot, where we were able to talk in a more relaxed setting. I asked Liam to tell me something about his journey and his life.

"I would say that the Church I was ordained into, the

243

Church that I decided to become a minister in, was a very, very different Church. It was fifteen years ago. The Church that I was ordained into was the Church that I felt I had come to serve. For the first number of years, I was the bride at every wedding and the corpse at every wake. You fit into a system and you do whatever you're asked to do. It isn't easy for the individual to stand back and go to the edge a little bit and ask, 'Is this what I really want to do?' There are questions, really, that many people didn't ask because you signed up, so you delivered.

"I would say that I had one epiphany in my life. I was chaplain in a psychiatric hospital. One evening, it was 5 o'clock, I came out of the hospital. The whole world and all its problems were weighing very heavily on my shoulders, and I also found it very difficult to distance myself from everything around me. I wasn't being sustained in the way I wanted to be, because I truly wasn't being truthful with myself. I wasn't being creative and using the gifts that I have. So I took a drive in my car, and I drove up into the hills that are overlooking the town, and I sat and played a piece of music that I had come across by John Michael Talbot. I was so really profoundly affected in that moment. The stars were coming out, and I was looking across the valley. The town that had really gotten to me was just a speck in the distance, so it could be a very good overall view. But what I really wondered about was that God could use somebody like John Michael Talbot to create such a beautiful song and a beautiful prayer experience for me, and I cried. I cried because he was doing what I'd love to do. In one sense, looking back now, it's like God heard me. It's ironic that ten years afterwards, I was to spend time with John Michael Talbot. But instead of listening to his music, I listened to questions. He just wanted to keep asking questions about the Celtic Spirit, and the music, and all of that kind of thing. It's so interesting, because once I had an experience of crying listening to music, and now people are having the same experience hearing my music. And I think one of the reasons that it's happened to me is because in some way I did have the courage to go to the edge, and jump off. The problem with this is that many of the clergy have been there, have gone to the edge... OK? But they jumped off in a different direction. Y'understand? I'm not saying this as a criticism, but I'm saying it as a fact.

"I grew up in a home which was a very, very conservative Catholic home. My father had come from down in

Cork. And in some way, it was in later years, I think that upbringing kind of nurtured, maybe, a respect of the tradition, and the beauty of the tradition. There was always music. My grandmother was a sean-nos singer, an old singer, singer of the old country music. She and two other girls would go around to all the wakes and weddings and they were hired out to sing. And at another stage... my grandfather was sixteen when he emigrated from Cobh. It was a beautiful story told about when all the people came to see them off. And he played the concertina. As they were leaving, in the small boat to go out to the liner, my grandfather started playing 'God Save Ireland.' And all the people on the boat started to sing. But so also did the people who were on the pier. Two years afterwards, he came back... he was one of the few who came back. And my mother said as there was music, my father moved up to the midlands where there was work, and so was music. So I was surrounded by music in one sense. It was there in the genes.

"I had always been interested in the spiritual life, but I was trying to find a creative way to pray, and I think that somehow the Irish tradition is a very natural tradition of spirituality, and the music. Everything gets married just at the right time. When I started writing, there was a niche there that hadn't been filled. A group like Clannad had something magical about their music, and it was spiritual-based, there's no doubt about it, but it was more of a secular market. And I thought, let's look at this in a more spiritual setting. Why can't we have the bodhrans in the church? They were there long before... Why can't we use the harps? They were the first instruments in the country. Why do we have to kind of anglicize, in one sense, our tradition, when we have the most beautiful elements in it? And one of the things I discovered also is that the people I gathered around to play had never an experience like this in church before, 'cause the first settings were churches. The concerts were a later development. And I had no problem getting musicians. One of the things I've discovered now, as the music moves all around the country, in small pockets, in all kinds of places—to the Aran Islands, to convents, to hospitals, to prisons—that obviously sometimes it's saying something, or it's touching something. And what I think it is... I remember one night—let me tell you the story— it was in a concert, and an old man started crying. He was quite visible and quite audible, and I thought, oh my God, I've upset him. So when it was over, we kind of met halfway, I was going to apologize to him, and he said, 'I'm really sorry.' I said, 'What's wrong? Have I upset you?' And he said, 'No, no, no. I haven't cried for years and years and years. When that drone started, it just touched something inside me. The only thing I can say is that it must have been my Celtic psyche. It released an awful lot for me.' So I think what I want to say to that is: number one, that's what liturgy should be about, a place of meeting, God and ourselves, in our most vulnerable places, so there's, hopefully, a natural progression to healing... insomuch as we recognize our brokenness. And secondly, that we can do it in a setting that is secure, and is familiar, and is non-threatening—for the Lord to do that—and we give ourselves the permission. The Irish people are not good at this at all. We don't allow ourselves to grieve, y'know, like other traditions do. So I think then the progression from there was that there was something in this that should be captured and should be worked at. But I have to say this as well, that I could not divorce it at all from the actual roots of the spirituality. And what do I mean by the roots of the spirituality? There are two things. There's what they call Celtic Spirituality, and there's Irish Spirituality. Celtic Spirituality is something you can get in many books, from a New Age stand, from Borders, to Hong Kong.

There's a bit of magic and there's a bit of shamanism. There's a bit of all kinds of stuff: druidism, paganism, you name it. Irish Spirituality is very different, because Irish Spirituality is based on the lives of the generations of people who went before us, who brought the Christian message to us, who in some way probably respected the Druidic tradition because some of the traditions still exist. For example, Ireland and Scotland are the only countries in the world that have the August bank holiday weekend which goes back to Lughnasa. OK, you've heard of Dancin' at Lughnasa? It was a festival 'cause of the harvest. The harvest was gathered, the harvest was going to be gathered, and it was a time of celebration, of comin' together. It's still kept! So they embrace some of the cultures that have come down through the centuries.

"But the Irish Spirituality, particularly, is reflected in the lives of the saints, the holy men and women, the thousands of hermits who lived once in the valley of Kevin at Glendalough; the lives of all the local saints in the local areas who set up the hospitals, the poorhouses, the churches. St. Lasarian was the local saint who brought Christianity to Leinster, who I did a first work on. Normally translated into Irish is going to be lasa, lasarian. The word 'lasa'... light. But the local people

249

never called him Lasarian; they called him Malasa. When you break down that it means, 'ma-lasa—my light.' And the name St. Lasarian survives today throughout the country. This is Irish Spirituality. Now, someone can go through the penitential stuff, difficulty, and all of that. But I think this is the kind of spirituality that is our Celtic Spirituality.

"For me, prayer is perpetual, and how do you stop the prayers of generations? I think it's only natural, it's part of our psyche, it's part of who we are, it's part of our spirit. So when they hear a melody, or they hear some song, 'cause many people have said, 'I've heard it somewhere before.' Of course you heard it before! And it's not because it's been written before. But in some way it's carried down through the generations. Maybe a note formation, maybe a triplet, the three notes... something like that. But I think we've got to a stage now that the more Europeanized it becomes, the more organized it becomes, and more complex. One city becomes the same as another. So how do you protect the ethnic? But unfortunately, the Church probably has lost out over the years and discarded all the beautiful artifacts and the treasures into the museums.

"For example, just take one tradition... the tradition

of the Anam Cara, the soul friend. It's so alive. And I know in the States, it's there as well. And what about therapy? Y'know? To do the same thing that was in the tradition, except that the tradition was a spiritually based one. There's a lot of traditions like that.

"I s'pose another thing I would say is that the more economically viable we are becoming, the more complex society is. Now, the Celtic tradition is not a complex one. It is a lot simpler, in means, in living... in prayer, even. And that's one of the reasons for the drive to live a more simple life. If you look at the spirituality of prophets, especially the desert fathers, you see a lot of similarities... the silence, which is really a bad word today! Y'know what I mean? For example, there's been a drive in the country to create sacred spaces within the Church and within our homes, and within the schools. At least it's a recognition that once again we need to find the sacred spaces in our lives...

"Another whole area is care for the environment. Now, you can get Greenpeace and the whole care for the environment. Fine. But it has to be God-centered as well. In the ancient Irish tradition, it *was* God-centered, because it was seen that we were given the earth to nurture as a gift. So there are a whole lot of areas that we

251

need to develop, I think, in our spirituality. The Church hasn't been good on this. They're so interested in morality—who slept with who and all this kind of stuff. D'ya know what I mean?"

"What hopes do you have for the future?"

"I think I would have hopes for my work, and hopes for the Church. I think with the Church, the first thing would be that there would be a maturing of faith. The sad reality is that many, many very intelligent people who hold very high-profile jobs have an infantile experience of their faith, right across the board. So that in some way we can in the Church present, in an imaginary way—or rather, in a creative way—the Gospel story. And that we realize that there's a technological age surrounding us and that we should be in there, giving them Mass as well. There was a talk a while back given by Mary Macdalese. She was talking to people who were involved in Christian broadcasting. And she said, 'I have a brother, my youngest brother, who is profoundly deaf. When I was growing up, sometimes when we would sit at the family table for a meal, and there would be all chatting going on. And suddenly,' she said, 'my brother would tug at my elbow, to tell me, look, I'm here. Don't forget that I'm here.' And she said that is our job today—as ministers and people who are involved in broadcasting—that we have to be 'tuggers at the elbows of society.' To say, look, we are here, and Christ is here, and don't forget it. I think that's what we should be doing in the Church, in a non-judgmental, non-threatening, non-authoritarian way. Let's face it. In Ireland, many of the people who were commissioned with authority and power are pre-Vatican II people. There are many, many situations throughout the country that for them Vatican II didn't even happen... in decision-making, in the role of women, in the proper place of liturgy, in the understanding of liturgy, in the use of resources, in the provision of resources. Asking the question 'is imagination and creativity dead or alive?' Or, 'does imagination and creativity cut across or interfere with my week, and if so, how does it?' Y'know, there are a lot of questions... like where my energy is turned: 'how am I sustained and where am I sustained from?'

"Another great tradition in Ireland is the Holy Well, where people went for healing, for blessing of cattle, and crops. Now, the wells are still there, but a lot of them are dry and have become overgrown because people aren't

253

lookin' after 'em...

"I can't write unless I pray. Now, this might sound absolutely crazy when I say this. But sometimes, for example, if I was doing the work on Patrick, or maybe the work on Edmund Rice. I imagine that he's sitting before me, and just saying, 'well, look, you don't need to be praised from where you are now. But I'm sure you want the Lord and His creation to be praised. But I want to do it in the way you want and is best, so somewhere we have to co-create together. You can co-create through me, and with me, and by me.' It's the same with Patrick. I really believe in what I call a co-creative spirituality, that the Lord can co-create through us and with us. I just think that if we could believe this, I think we could change.

"My hope would be that I would keep, in some way, inspiring people... touching people in some way, enabling them to find a space, but in particularly, enabling them to be part of their heritage. That's not saying there's a lot in our heritage that we shouldn't be proud of. But we can choose to be resentful and bitter, or we can choose to embrace the weaknesses as well, and we can learn from them. For example, the Famine. One question that became very striking for me was why did *my* ancestors survive? What means did they use to survive? Why should my ancestors survive, and somebody else's not? So in that sense, y'know, I think you have to embrace both.

"And there are times I find it very difficult. I find it a lonely place to be... misunderstood sometimes... angry sometimes... because, I don't know, you feel kind of... I have something good here, why can't everybody else believe it as well? D'ya know what I mean? You really have to believe in what you're doing, and get behind it.

"Ask me where I'll be in five years' time, I have no idea. I really have no idea... I travel quite a lot to the States. One thing I do know is I can't be cut off for too long. What do I mean by that? I think, basically, you can be in a parish in the States or in a parish in Ireland. There's no difference, except if you scratch the surface, I think. Y'know, so many American people are so proud of their heritage. And I'm not talking about shamrocks and shalalees now, but I'm talking about those who are searching it for themselves, as you've talked about. 'Cause many people are searching for meaning in life, and they recognize that meaning and spirituality is *this* place" *(gesturing to his heart.)* "And that is not saying that there is not a lot of pain and a lot of hurt, abuse, and a lot of anger within the Church. But it's good that in the past few years, the boil has been lanced in some way. The problem is when it is lanced, what's going to be there to support the structures to show people that there is a depth in our spirituality, and not everybody is bad?

"One thing that saddens me is that, well, maybe I'm too young at it yet. What I mean, at composing. But I don't see many people coming behind me. I just don't. That's not to sound in any way condescending. That's the first thing. Secondly, I would say that..." *(Pause.)* "I think these years are crucial. If the Church now would listen, and get its place in order... What do I mean by getting the Church in order? I think the first thing the Church needs to do is to start putting resources into people, and not into buildings, and not into institutions. I think that would be my experience. And that the liturgy is the one meeting place where we still meet a lot of our people. Let's make it worthwhile for them." *(Pause.)* "Easier said than done..."

(The rain was pounding onto the roof of the car, almost drowning out our voices.)

"In the meantime, I have a great time goin' around

the country!" *(Laughter.)* "I think people are great. I really do. I'm going to Northern Ireland next week for a workshop.

"You have to have a sense of humor as well. That was very important in the Irish tradition. To be able to laugh at ourselves and have a sense of humor. I think that's important.

"I think the Lord provides as well. He's provided for me. He's helped me in many a crisis. The Lord provides. He does really… but I'm in a hurry!" *(Laughter.)* "I can say, 'I know you're looking after me, but…'

"Let me play a piece of music for you. It's written for the people of Omagh… *'The Silence and the Sorrow.'* I think out of silence something beautiful can come. This piece of music is based on the Pieta, where Mary holds Jesus. The girl who recorded this, her brother was paralyzed just before the recording. So it was very fitting for her to do this. I think it was a healing in itself. I certainly believe that… let's listen to it."

(We sat and listened to the piece of music.)

"I think there are many, many women in Northern Ireland who could write this. And so many people were

257

crying when they heard it. And y'know, it's a privileged place to be, to be able to do that. Not that I in any way gloat over that people cry... It's a gift to cry. I remember one night, the Edmund Rice Story. I did a piece called, 'Pity Them the Child.' I worked with a group of children in a deaf and dumb school. I got them to come and do the song with me. And I deliberately put an oboe solo in the middle of it because when the singing stopped and the oboe played, the children could just stand there. It was kind of reflecting the way we can just cut people out. But the main theme of the song is to address the whole issue of child abuse and all that. It is a privileged place to be, to try to provide, to encourage them to a space where it is painful. But it's out of pain that beauty can be born.

"You've asked me about hope... The other night, near Limerick, when young people come up to you after a concert and say, 'I was very moved by that.' That's where hope lies..." *(Another pause.)* "I'm better at writing and singing than I am at giving interviews..." *(A warm smile.)*

"In a time when Celtic music has come to prominence, the name of Liam Lawton is becoming well

258

known in liturgical music circles. From Ireland, Liam has been composing music in the Celtic idiom for numerous years. Two of his collections have been used for two major television broadcasts shown throughout Europe. He writes both in the native Gaelic language and also in English in the traditional style. In his work, Liam has given life to the great and beautiful history of Ireland, using the ancient prayers and traditions as the main source of his texts. Fr. Lawton is a priest of the Diocese of Kildare and Leighlin, and is currently on the staff of Saint Patrick's College, Carlow. One of his recent collections from GIA is entitled Ancient Ways, Future Days."   *GIA*

SOMETIMES A STAR...

ðazzling, ðazzling beyonð ðazzle...

Michael was retired, in his late sixties, married, with grown children and grandchildren. For years he had been a steel worker and was employed at the pharmaceutical plant nearby. Michael had the face of an angel, a demeanor filled with light. There was such a genuine humility that seemed to emanate from him. At first he was very hesitant to speak. He thought he wasn't very good with words, but once he got going, he sounded more and more like a true poet! I would go as far as to

261

say he was a mystic and a visionary.

"I mostly grew up appreciatin' the life around us. Nowadays there are a lot of things happening that we don't like. I don't like divorce, actually, as well as abortion. I'm against abortion. I've noticed the younger people that are going to church, they like to participate more in it. You have these changing movements. They're not my cup of tea. I prefer a cup of coffee, as the case may be! It's good, too, I s'pose. A lot of it brings the Spirit more into their lives—the Holy Spirit. But I find in my own spirituality now, I've been careless at times, but I found a new spirituality within the last number of years. I wouldn't say it was a new spirituality, but it's… it's… it's a devotion more to Our Lady. I don't go directly to Our Lord. I do everything through Mary. It's a type of true devotion. I try to do it. I fail naturally enough. You might find that new or not, do ya?"

"No, not really. It seems to be something that's happening more and more now."

"Yeah. That's right. I do everything through Our Lady. I won't ask Jesus directly. I'll ask Him through

262

her. Like in the Eucharist now, when we receive the Eucharist, it's like... it was through Mary that Jesus came into the world. When we receive Him in Holy Communion, I feel it's through Our Lady I'm receivin' Him. Y'know? And I find a great fulfillment in that, since I have that devotion. I'm not putting her above Jesus or anything like that, but it's a way to Him... like in everything I do, I find that. Going back twenty years, I had devotion to her already. But it's not perfect in me yet.

"I find that as I'm getting older now, I'm drawn more to Our Lady. I find I have to go to her to get to Him. And I find... I find nothin' wrong with it. I find I'm very fulfilled in it, and I find consolation. Goin' through life, we all get crosses and things, and I find that cross is lightened because of her. Many cares in my life... like with my daughter now, leavin' the Church. I found it hard to accept that. And still, even to this day, I hope she'll come back. I'm not givin' up. And it mightn't be in my lifetime. But I have faith and confidence enough in Our Lady—to Jesus, through Our Lady—that she'll come back. I know we all have to search for the truth. Everyone is expected to search for the truth. Some mightn't find it in the Catholic Church, and find it in some other church."

"How old is your daughter? And when did she go to the other church?"

"She's about twenty-three, and it's about six years ago, I s'pose. She left, and she went back again. I still have hope. It's all right if she finds Jesus through that ch... I reckon it's a cult, I think. I still have faith in her that she'll come back." *(And almost in a whisper:)* "'Cause she was born that way... eh, born a Catholic. I find it hard to express myself, but you know what I mean?"

"You're doing fine. Yes, I know what you mean."

(Softly) "Yeah. But that's one thing. Like in other things that would happen in our lives, to have confidence in Jesus at all times, never failing, because if you doubt Him, you're failing, if you know what I mean...

"So I hope that brings somethin' to light to you."

"Yes, thank you. How about when you were younger? Is this something that's grown, your spiritual-

264

ity, over the years?"

"It has grown. But then at the same time, it has waned a bit in between as well, like... But I'm more conscious of it now, even though, like, there would be frailty. At the same time it's a constant, it's a constant, um, effort. And I find the more a person tries to be spiritual or holy, the greater the temptation. I find that. In other words, I am more conscious of the devil now. Well, I've been conscious of him all the time, but I'm more conscious of him now than I have been. Like, this day and age, a lot of people don't, uh... don't think he exists. Which he is, very much alive, unfortunately. How do you find that?"

(I nodded, and he continued.)

"That's why we should put greater effort into trying to be holy, but at the same time, the more holy a person tries to be, as I said, the greater they're going to get the temptation. Maybe not all people, but some people. Because he knows... the Devil knows. The people that are going around humdrum from day to day, he says, 'Oh, they're OK, they're safe enough.' But the one that constantly tries to be holier, he goes after them especially. Now, that's my thinking of it. You have to be very careful, because y'know, you think you're gettin' holy, and at the same time you might be tricked into thinkin' that you are gettin' holy. We have to trust in the Lord."

"Can you tell me something about your upbringing?"

"Well, my father and mother were Catholics. Goin' back as far as I can, there were Catholics, goin' back a couple of hundred years. My mother was a holy woman. My father, well, he wasn't; he wasn't a holy man, but there were times that he would be.

"I have five brothers and one sister. They're not extraordinary, they just try to be, y'know, Christians, like... How shall I put it... they're not as conscious of prayin' as I am, I'll put it that way. In their own way they try to be holy, but it's just ordinary, if you know what I mean."

After a rather long pause, I asked if he had regular times in the day to pray.

266

"I do. Lately now, if I wake early in the morning... I believe that when you wake, no matter what time, you should praise God. And sometimes when I wake I will say the Rosary, and I don't ask for any request in sayin' that Rosary. I say the Rosary just to praise God. We're inclined to look for petitions when we pray, which is a good thing, but that shouldn't be our chief reason. It should be to praise God at all times, even when we go to bed at night time, thank Him for all the graces and benefits He bestowed upon us during our whole life..."

"Or even just for the day..."

"For the day. That's right. It's like, if we're lookin' at the day now, we should say it's a grand day, thank God, and if it's not a good day, well, it's a grand day anyway!" (*Another hesitation.*) "Well, uh, I hope that's givin' you somethin'..."

"It's very helpful, yes. Michael, do you have grandchildren?"

"I only just have two grandchildren, one from earlier and one just this year. They're my first grandchildren."

"Looking ahead, in this new millennium, if you were to leave them the kind of Church that you would like, what would it be?"

"For the grandchildren, is it?"

"What would you say to your grandchildren as they're growing up?"

"Well, I would like them to be charitable to people, and praise the Lord, as I say. That would actually be the first thing. And they also have a soul, and that you must look after it. We have to have food, for eat and drink to sustain the body. We also have a soul and we must sustain that too, by the Holy Communion. That's the food for the soul. I'd try to tell them that... I would be very conscious that they would know about the soul. What's a hundred years compared to eternity!" *(He paused, and then he spoke more quickly and more animatedly.)* "But I'd like to get it conveyed to them in a cheerful type of way, in a kind of, uh... not 'you must do this and you must do that', you know... to try to get them to love, to do a thing out of love, rather than because you have to. That applies to us all, I s'pose. There was a Rule of St.

Augustine. He used to say, 'Before all things, brother, we must love God first, because He first loved us.' The bishop was saying Mass here this morning, and he was sayin' that God is searching for us. We search for God, and God is searching for each one of us, He loves us so much. If we could convey the love that God has for us toward each other, it would be great, in this world of strife. And down through the ages, the Church went through its dark history as well, y'know, persecution and all. And I s'pose that we'll have more persecution. There'll be lots of things... but, uh... God has to triumph in the end. I feel that confident about it. You might say you have to face reality to think things are getting worse and worse. But we don't know the mind of God...

"There seems to be an awful lot of materialism in the world. And greed. And things like that. The Celtic Tiger... where is Christ? You could be pessimistic, too, about the way things are happening, from a spiritual point of view. We might get wealth, all right; if the two of them could go along side by side, it would be great. I mean to say, there's an awful lot of things happenin', since we all could err that way. It's like St Paul says, 'There but by the grace of God goes I.' We could be the one that he's talking about. And I think the Church is

269

very much hurt today.Well, in a sense the people and a certain number of the clergy have fallen. But they're just an individual member of the Church. The Church as a whole doesn't, doesn't fall. 'Tis the members. That's where people get mixed up. It's the members who fall. They're only human. You'd be inclined to put them and the Church all together."

"And some are inclined to turn away, turn their backs to the Church, when it's the individuals that are gone astray."

"That's right. It's like sayin' 'everyone is charitable.' Same brush, then!" *(Quick laugh.)* "How have you found it here now? The people? Are a lot of people taken up with the problems, with so many problems, shall we say, trying to live with sickness and everything, that it's hard to be spiritual, too, in that sense, I s'pose? I know it's tough on young people. But they're in a different age, they're in a different age, ya see..."

"I know, a lot of them are not going to church. I wonder, where are they being nourished? Where are they being sustained..."

270

"Yes..."

"What replenishes them? Do they find God some-where else? So those are some of the questions... What would you ask them? If you were talking with a young person right now, what would be one or two of the things you might say, or ask them? Maybe a young person who said, 'I'm not going to church anymore.' What would you say?"

"Well, I'd say to them, um... I'd say you're putting your soul in grave danger. I'd say that to them. I'd like to be in a position to be able to talk to them without talking *at* them." *(He smiled.)* "I'm the type of a person... I can be hasty at times, and mightn't be able to speak rightly to them.

"I'm a bit concerned about their soul, I s'pose. It's like, to convey it in words that is meaningful to them. Now, looking at my own. They go to church and all that. They're lookin' at things different than I would. A few of my daughters are living in Dublin. I get on with them. I get on with all my family. But, you see, if you mention religion to some, it's taboo, like they just switch off. How can you get across that? All the people now, like

271

yourself, you'd have a way of conveying the truth. It's like being a teacher. But for your ordinary person, how can you convey it, the true meaning, to them? Nowadays, I think you have to be very skillful to be able to do that. And another thing is, I think you mightn't be able to do it by words, but you could do it by actions... if you try to lead a good life. We don't know, but along the line somewhere it might click. Like they might say there must be somethin' in it. When you're goin' through your life they mightn't change, but when you're dead and gone, they might say, well, your father or your mother tried to live a good life... there must be somethin' in it. They might, and they might not, of course!" *(Short laugh.)* "I think example is a great thing. It's better than tellin' 'em. Example. A good example. As I say, it speaks louder than words."

"Young people go through stages. I know I did. And I'm sure you did..."

"I did, yes."

"And very often when they hit their thirties, they come back. The Fundamentalist Church in America is

quite big right now. And some people's fear is, yes, that it's a cult. What I've seen, in most places, it's not. I've asked questions and talked with people. Why did they leave the churches they grew up in? And many times they'll say because they felt a sense of warmth and love and acceptance in the so-called 'born-again' churches. They were not feeling that in the traditional churches. It's not just Catholic. Protestant, Catholic... all of the main-line traditional churches in America."

"Well, I went to that church where my daughter was. I can't say I was comfortable with it, but at the same time, they seemed to have a great, uh... There was a lot of hymn-singing, y'know. I think they do feel that they're attached to others, all within the group. They seem to have a bond... a whale of a bond! Whereas, like, well... there are a lot of numbers in our church, and they don't get so close to each other, if you know what I mean. Close in the sense, like, that they're community. They seem to be very much together..." *(Long pause.)* "I don't know how to put it. But they seem to have a great respect for each another, anyway. I find that. And maybe that's what draws them." *(Another long pause.)* "They put you to shame sometimes... in the sense that

273

those of us that are in the established churches, we're going on our own way. Like with us, when you go to a service, you're at a church service, then you go through your own everyday life. But then you meet some of these, they seem to live with each other. Even when they leave their service, some of them go and stay in the same accommodations for twenty-four hours a day, y'know. I don't think you'd have time to breathe, in a sense... Space. You have to have space. Like when you go to your own room at night. I like to be alone there, and try to see God there as well."

"Having some time alone with God."

"Alone with God... that's it. That's wonderful. And to combine prayer. Is that more helpful, like...to God?"

"Oh I think God appreciates any time we can give to Him! It really doesn't matter how we pray. Whatever way that's comfortable..."

"It's hard, to find out. And then you question your-self, are you doin' the right thing at times. You think you might be doing the right thing, but... It's like, how can you get people back into the church... the established church?" *(And another long pause.)* "But we have to have love for each other then. There's an awful lot of hatred around. Like with the wars going on at the moment. In my own thinking, just look at it. Why is there war? It gradually comes down to the home. You'll eventually get back to 'why is there war in a country?' Why is there one country against another? And eventually it goes back straightway, it goes back to the home. If there's a grievance in the home, you must try and live with each other, and uh, be forgiving. We all fail in that respect, sometimes. If there were peace and harmony in the home, like you would have peace in the world. It starts in the home. It's the nucleus, like. I find if we could do that, it'll overflow onto the streets, the towns, the countries..."

"Sounds good to me. And it might be a good moment to stop, too! Thank you, Michael."

"Thanks awfully. Hope I haven't bored you too much."

"Oh, no... far from it."

When Michael was leaving, we were chatting briefly, saying that it's important to have both sides of the story, even criticism. And I said, 'You know, in all our lives there may be a time of doubt and criticism, but it is often just a stage we are going through. This can help us understand others when they have fallen away, so to speak.'

We moved into the kitchen, and while washing out his teacup, he continued in a reflective vein.

"You were saying, we can see the glory of God in everything..."

"You can see the glory of God in everything. You need only to look around! Even in a weed, which is a flower of course. It's glory to God! And even the smallest insect. It's wonderful. Even goes down to microscopic things. 'Cause only God could have made these!" *(Michael turned to look out the window and, quite animated, he continued:)* "Look out there, now... you can see clouds, and the land is stretchin' there, and stretchin' here" *(gesturing with his hands)* "...and there's water in between, and there's an island in between. Well, it's like the hands of God enfoldin' the world. That's only in this

276

area now. If you apply that to...

"Y'know... you can see it, everywhere. 'Tis wonderful. The Glory of God, seen in the things around us. It will help us..." *(quick laugh)* "...to see the things that are hard or distasteful, when you see God in everything. And even suffering. We have to take some sufferin' too. God Himself suffered, on the Cross. I remember one time I had a stroke, the hand and face. I was up in hospital, and God took life out of me. I couldn't move that hand. Then one day, the feeling came back into my hand. And at that instant it struck me that God takes life but also gave my life back as well. Maybe events in your life, too, would you maybe be conscious of that. And that's another reason for being thankful to God. Wonderful. Overcoming sickness. I got a wonderful feeling. He brought the life back into me. God was giving me new life! There was a message in it for me... to amend my life, and to lead a better life. You get more awareness of things around you that you were not aware of before, and you begin to appreciate them better. Maybe an event in your life, too, would make you be conscious of that. And that's another reason for being thankful to God... y'know... overcomin' sickness."

"Yes, and looking back over our lives and seeing where God got us through rough times..."

"Yeah. Because, as I see it... we've got a body, but what's more important is we've got a mortal soul. And there's nothing more beautiful than a soul, and, and a state of grace... 'tis, 'tis dazzlin'..." *(Short laugh)* "Dazzling beyond all dazzle!"

"Yes, Michael, it is dazzling, isn't it!"

"...uh, just some of my thoughts, anyway, Sister."

I saw some light at the end of the tunnel...

Katherine was a woman in her mid-fifties, married, with four children. Before she was married she was a teacher in the primary grades. We met in a coffee shop where she was working at the time. I asked her if she could say something about her relationship with God and the Church.

"I'm just trying to think... My concept of God, really, is what I want to say. As a small child, I loved God more than Jesus, I think. God was always number one for me. When I went to school, God was removed to one

279

side, and Jesus was put in His place. I kind of felt there was something wrong with that. I think the Roman Catholic religion puts Jesus too much forward. I know we believe in the Trinity, but yet I still felt that God is the One Person which we'd have as a priority, and we didn't."

"Where did you find God, when you were a child... or sense God?"

"As a child? Within me... He was in there somewhere. If I wanted to talk to somebody, it was Him. I purposely would look for Him. I could see Him everywhere, in fact. Except, can't see Him in Jesus. I feel somethin's blocking me. There's a block there. I always felt that God to me was like a comforting person. Went to school. Couldn't wait to go to school 'cause I had this insatiable need to learn. I went into a school with nuns who were nasty, horrible, and totally guilt-ridden, and ended up making me totally guilt-ridden as well. That's when the conflict began. I said to myself, if God is nice, why are the Brides of Christ so nasty? Ya see? And I thought there's something wrong here. These were women who said they had a vocation and that they were

280

special. They were the special ones chosen by God and they answered the call. And yet, they were mean to the people around them. Very strange. I remember a nun actually beating a child, and I thought to myself, there's something seriously wrong here. As a child it made an impression, at the age of four. I'll give you an example of what happened to me…

"In Lent, in Ireland, you went off sweets, you didn't eat sweets, you didn't eat ice cream, you didn't eat anything. I was five, I think, and I ate an ice cream during Lent. And a nun saw me eating an ice cream. I came into school the following morning, and she said, 'Get up on the table.' I stood on the table, and she came down and lashed my back. And she said, 'This girl is to be punished because she ate an ice cream during Lent.' Nobody had ever slapped me before. I jumped off the table, and to this day, I can still visualize that huge door. I dragged the door open, and ran down to my grandmother. Now my grandmother was a very strong Irishwoman. Very tall, stood very straight, and she said, 'Right, that does it.' She took off her apron, rolled up her sleeves, and she said, 'I'm goin' up to see them.' And up she went. But y'see, it made it all the worse, because if your mother or someone representing you complained,

281

you were actually ridiculed and treated badly from there on. And that's what happened. Very, very sad situation, really. My school was appalling. Not so much for me in a sense, but for the children that they abused. And they did. Very sad.

"I remember on another occasion, we were in first class. First class was First Communion. And the priest was coming to visit us. It was a major hassle when the priest came, because everything had to be polished, everything had to be perfect. And we were to be examined. And the head teacher who was examining us, we were absolutely terrified of her because she had a stick with splintery wood. And she had the stick waiting. If you didn't answer your question, you were gone. The question was, 'Who is God?' and 'Who made the world?' We were taught to learn all this stuff out of the Catechism with no explanation. When I was a child, I had to have an explanation. You can imagine how I felt, because here am I, listening to all this stuff, and I'm asking in my own head, what does this mean? And I couldn't ask the nun what it meant because she wouldn't tell me, 'cause that was the Roman Catholic religion—you did not question. So, I came into class in the mornin', and she started. We were in a line, and before she got to me, I wet my pants. So she selected one of the orphans to go out and bring in the rags and clean up my mess. And that hurt me even more than the actual wetting of my pants because I couldn't right it. I did the mess, but that poor girl had to clean it up...

"So, as the years moved on, I had the guilt... you see, this guilt thing we grew up with, the Roman Catholic guilt. And yet inside in my mind thinking it wasn't the God that I knew. Something's wrong here, something seriously wrong. Then, within my family... My parents didn't go to Mass. It was in the 1950's. It was a most unusual thing, and in a small town like this, you just didn't speak about that. And every Sunday, there were the two of us—my mother, who was just as strong-willed as my grandmother, but wouldn't go to Mass. My mother would call in to the cathedral, check to see what priest said the Mass, and then we'd go up to my grandmother's. The first thing, we'd go in the door, and my grandmother would say 'good morning,' 'how are you' or whatever. And then she'd say, 'And Peggy, who said Mass?' and my mother would say Father So-and-so. And my grandmother would think we had gone to Mass. Then I went into school the following morning, and the teacher, the nun, would say, 'Who said Mass?' And everybody would say whatever Mass we were at. And then she would ask what happened in the Gospel. Of course, I didn't know that because..." *(Short laugh.)* "...I wasn't at Mass! But still then, behind all of that, I wanted to worship God. My parents didn't, because they had their own reasons for that. My grandmother did, but it was an austere type of strict religion. Of course, she was used to that framework. I was in the middle. I wanted to worship God in my way, and I couldn't. So I hid it all up, and became quite introverted in the end. It went on and on and on...

"Then it came to confirmation. Confirmation rituals. The same thing all over again... the 'slapper' was out if you didn't answer. You had the examination by the priest. I remember going to the Confirmation Mass. It should have been a great day, but it was a horrific day for me. My parents came, but I knew they didn't want to be there. But they were my family, so they came. They got nothing, absolutely nothing out of it. All I can remember is swinging back, and practically fainting at that point in time because we weren't allowed to eat. We had to fast. That was my confirmation. Nothing memorable about it at all...

"After that, went on to secondary school. Continued

on again, the same rituals, and the nuns again, the guilt. At this point in time, though, we got onto the makeup story. If you were a Roman Catholic girl, you did not wear makeup, because if you did, you were going to Hell and the worms would eat your face, anyway. That's what we were told! So, we thought, gee, this is weird, all the other girls are wearing makeup. What's the story here? So, we said this can't be right. Went into fifth year, and we were in what you'd call the hormonal stage of life. And we were very interested in boys... and madly in love with Elvis Presley and people like that. One of my friends, who was quite outspoken, decided she was going to ask the crucial question. So she asked the sister, 'Did Joseph ever kiss Mary?' The nun went swooping from the top of the classroom down and lashed out into the girl's face. My friend was thrown out of the class, and we were all still sitting there, gob-smacked, knowing full well that she was going to slap her anyway. But we were still there thinking... did he ever kiss her? We never found out the answer to that story... We also wanted to know, did Jesus have brothers and sisters? And nobody would answer that question either.

"Continued on... Never read the Bible. Very vague Bible-reading situation. And that's something I wanted

285

to read, because to me they were the stories, they were the background to what I was believing in. Then I had another problem. I had a lot of Church of Ireland friends, and I wasn't supposed to have them. Because where I lived was just below the actual Church of Ireland building. So, they were all my friends. My uncles on my mother's side all worked for what we would call the Anglo-Irish. So I would have had an English kind of influence, there would have been an Irish influence, I would have had a 'we hate the Pope' influence, and 'we hate Republicans' influence as well. Kind of a bit of a melting pot, really. But at the end of the day, I think it helped me to realize that everybody was equal. Whereas, other people still believed we are the one true Church..., 'you will not be saved without becoming a Roman Catholic,' 'you follow the Church of Rome.' But I didn't...

"When I came to college, I decided, right, I'm opting out. So I left going to Mass... I didn't have to go anymore. But the odd thing was, when I went to college in Cork, I went to Mass up there. I went to the Franciscan Church, and I got so much solace from them. Oh, I did... I went in, and these men were talking from a different level than what I would call the diocesan parish-type priest. I was up there, they didn't know me, I didn't know them, and I listened to what they had to say. Well, if they could have listened to my old priests... because they were preachin' one thing, and doing somethin' else. So as the years went by, anyway, I still had my love of God in here somewhere" *(Putting her hand near her heart).* "I could still talk to Him. And I thought to myself, but I haven't lost Him. And that was good...

"One year, the Redemptorists came to town. And I thought, we've nothing to do tonight, we could go to this and see what it's about. So we went up there, and there were two young priests. They were a breath of fresh air. I saw something in them that was something different. And I decided, right, I'll go to confession, and my sister went as well. Hadn't been to confession for years. I considered confession as being something not quite right. I felt, why can't we confess to Him in here somewhere?" *(Once again placing her hand on her heart.)* "Why do I have to tell this to somebody else, who knows nothing about me, and who might judge me anyway? My feeling was the one to judge me was God, and myself. So, went into confession, and the problem I had was... that any boy I ever dated only wanted one thing, and I didn't want to give it! So I went in and I poured it out to this guy,

287

'This is my problem here.' And I said, 'What am I going to do? I can't meet a man who wants me for my brain. There's something wrong. I want to meet a man who wants me for me, and the sex comes later.' So he said, 'You're unique' and I said, 'Really?' This was the '60s remember... 'twas the '60s, free love. We had it here too! And I said, 'What am I going to do?' He said, 'You probably will meet somebody eventually.' So he said, 'I'm not going to give you any penance,' because I wasn't up to saying Rosaries or Hail Marys, and these kind of things. So that was good. So I said then, 'what am I going to do then for my penance?' And he said, 'Would you have a pound?' and I said, 'I have.' And he said, 'Go to a telephone directory, find the name of an unmarried mothers' institution, and send them a pound. What would you think of that?' And I thought that sounds more reasonable to me. Then he said we'd correspond again. In the meantime, my sister was in the other box with another guy. And she came out and she said, 'This was enlightenment! I can't believe it. This guy is talking my lingo. We have an appointment later.' So I said, 'What do you mean?' 'He's comin' down to our house at 11 o'clock when he's finished hearing confessions.' Well, he came down, and he stayed with us the whole two weeks. He came every single night. He was comin' from the same spiritual place as we were. Totally frustrated with the Church. I saw some light at the end of the tunnel. Because I now found somebody in what I call the orthodox religion that I had been brought into who heard and listened to what I had to say. No guilt. Guilt didn't come into this; this was totally different.

"One of the times he was visiting us, we told him our parents were quite strict, and we wanted to go on holiday, and they wouldn't allow us. He said, 'Let's come up with a compromise and we'll work something out. Where would you like to go?' And we said, 'Anywhere, just anywhere, just to get away for a week.' Well, my father went to a school taught by Cistercian monks. Even though he gave up his religion, he kept up his connection with one of the monks up there. Because he said that was God, these guys... They had a totally different belief. They didn't have all the trappings of the guilt. They didn't have what we call the business side of our religion. He said these were men who gave up everything, went to God, and yet had sympathy and empathy with others. So, we explained this to the priest, and he asked, 'Have they got a retreat house?' And we said, 'They have, up on the county road.' 'Would your father

289

let you go up there? Would he trust the monks?' And we said, 'Maybe he might.' So we brought him to my father, and said, 'Dad, listen to what Father Peter has to say.' 'Look, they'll be safe up there. Would you let them go?' So Dad thought about it and said yes. So, we wrote to the Prior, who said yes, certainly come. Just one slight problem... the lady who ran the retreat house had a heart attack. And the only place they could stay is in a pub in the village. And we thought, 'OK, this is it!' And the monk continued, 'But they'll come up at nine in the morning and they'll stay all day and go back down.' So we went up.

We were... I think I was twenty and my sister was eighteen. We absolutely adored the place. It was wonderful. There was peace, tranquility. The next day, a priest came down, a monk, and introduced himself. And he got friendly with us, although he wasn't supposed to, because the monks were actually enclosed, apart from the few who dealt with the guests. Now, we wore miniskirts. It was the '60s, remember. Hot summer... Three days into the event, we were sent for by the Father Prior, to come to the parlor. And he said, 'Girls, we're very happy to have you here. But do you have any longer skirts by any chance? Because the monks are getting a little upset.' So we said, 'We're very sorry, but these are our skirts, and we're very sorry for upsetting the monks.' We were so innocent. We actually didn't understand we were really upsetting them, because we assumed that the monks were like eunuchs and they didn't have feelings like that! So we said, 'We have jeans, would they do?' And he said, 'They'll have to...' So we wore jeans, in the sweltering summer. But in the meantime, anyway, the priest that we befriended came every morning. Came up the driveway... he appeared. And one day he said, 'Will you come for a walk, it's a beautiful view.' And innocent as we were, we said 'yes'—we were like lambs to the slaughter—and we went with him. And he said stand up on the gate and you'll see better. And the next thing, his hands went up. We knew it was wrong, of course, and we said, 'Hey, what are you doing?' And years later we found out from someone else that this guy, his mother put him into the priesthood. He abused some-body, he was then shunted to the monastery, and he was moved again. We don't know where he is today. But we can well understand now why these guys do it. We have all this sympathy for them, understand. But a lot of it is due to the Irish mother syndrome. Very clearly it's there. A mother wanted to have maybe the prestige of a son

being within the situation. That was our experience anyway, there... But now, that didn't upset us as much as our
education within the Roman Catholic Church. And yet, I
came back and went to Mass from thereon. I actually
came back one hundred percent to worship, within the
church situation.

"Grew up, then. Got married. Married someone who
was ultra-conservative who came from a very conservative family. Found it quite difficult. He was always saying the Rosary, and me on the other side of the bed
talkin' to God in my head. Strange. Very strange thing.
And he would say to me, 'You're not prayin', are ya?'
And I'm in there communing with God, in my fashion,
prayin' for the guy on his knees, and praying for other
things. And yet, he thought I wasn't doing what I should
do. He believed in going to Mass every Sunday, regardless of how ill you felt, it didn't matter. I, on the other
hand, might say I don't feel like goin' today. And he
couldn't come to terms with that. But it gradually
changed, and he changed too. And he now will not go to
Mass if he doesn't feel like going, and if something
upsets him, he won't go to Mass either. We feel that the
Church is all right. The regime is the problem, and the
people who made the rules are the problem. God isn't

the problem. People say to me, 'How can you go to Mass even though you know there's hypocrisy there?' And I say to them, 'I'm goin' to Mass because I need to worship with others. I need to be with my own people. I go there, and I listen to what is said, the word of God. I don't listen to the homily unless I know that the guy who's giving the homily means it. And I know them so well, I know whether they mean it or they don't. So I just switch off with certain people, and I sit there and I'm with God and I'm there because I want to share Bread with Him, and I'm goin' there as a memorial to Him. Also... I don't really know if I believe in the True Presence, that it is the Body of Christ. I could be excommunicated for saying it, but I do believe it. I think somebody decided it along the way, but I don't think Jesus did. I think He sat with his friends, and He said to them, 'This is my Body and this is my Blood. Remember me.' Because anybody could get bread and anybody could get wine in those days. Not so much now, I s'pose. In our culture, you could get a cup of tea... it's similar. And He said, 'Will you remember me?' Maybe today you would give somebody a gift. This was His gift. I believe by taking the Bread and the Wine, you are bringing Him into you, and you are accepting it. That's real. He's your friend. He's the guy who's there. Is He the Son of God? That's another question... That's another problem that goes through my head. Was He really the Son of God? Or was He a very holy man with great intuition? I never met Him. But me, with my thoughts, I'm thinking... I'd love to meet Him. And my son feels the same way. I often said to my son, 'Who would you like to meet in life?' And he said to me, 'I'd like to meet Jesus Christ, Hitler,' and I think it was Mother Teresa, someone like that. And I said to him, 'Why?' 'Because,' he said, 'Mom, I need to see the guy. I need to look into His face, and then I'll know who He is.' And I feel that way myself. I do. I often think, God is God, but Jesus is somebody else. He came down here. He was human...

"And who was Mohammed? He's another one. Who's Buddha? Who were all these people? We never saw them. Did they really exist is another question... What would we know of that? But I believe God is left. That's the difference, and that's why Jesus is my problem. As a child I was made to love Jesus. I was told I had to love Him. You can't be made to love somebody. That's in here." *(Placing her hand on the heart.)* "You love someone from here. No one can tell you who you fall in love with. Nobody told me to fall in love with Eddie...

294

Fell in love with him, fell in love with me. If my mother said to me, you are to fall in love with Eddie, I wouldn't have done that for her. So, that's the conflict. That's resolved now, I think, to a certain extent, 'cause I feel comfortable now. Very comfortable. I really do. And God is there for me. He's everywhere. He's up there, He's in me—whatever. He's probably in the curtains as we sit here! And that's it. But, Jesus is the question, still... It's not a problem for me. Just like, people believe in Buddha, people believe in Mohammed. So, many might say 'Oh, you're goin' the wrong way.' That's where I'm heading. And that's why I have no problem talking to, sharing communion with, any other denomination. What bothers me, to a certain extent, are the people who have tunnel vision and can't really see. They're locked in that situation and they really haven't seen God yet. It's sad for me to see people like that. Why can't people see what I see, and how come *I* can see it? We all went through the same situation.

"I think all religion is a block to God. It is. And the Celts had it right. And I think I must be a Celt, sorting it out. Because they believed that the earth and God and themselves were one. Something that I love. Maybe I might have been a druid in a former life or something like that. But, y'know, they had it right. And what happened? They had it here…" *(Gesturing toward her heart again.)* "Roman Catholicism came… well, not Roman, no. Christianity came to Ireland. And Christianity took on the Celtic beliefs to a certain extent, and they switched around and they adapted to things. But then Roman Catholicism came, and that's where the problems started. Because Roman Catholicism is, I feel, a business. That's what it is. It's a power game. It's a personality game. The whole thing is power and personality, and control. That's what it is, control… And that's where all religion has gone wrong. That's why we have all the problems that we have today. We've priests who are totally confused; they don't know who they are or what they are. They're goin' around abusing women, because why? Because they have a natural inborn instinct to mate. Even God made us to mate. That was part of His plan. And we have a religion who tells a man that he can't do that. Wrong. Something's seriously wrong. It's a natural human instinct. It should be an instinct that you appreciate, and you say God gives us this. It can't be wrong. You don't abuse it. You don't abuse any privilege you get. I never say I'm a Roman Catholic. I say I'm a Christian. And I s'pose I could go beyond that even, if I could think of another word. Even the word 'Christian' isn't right for me, either, I s'pose, to a certain extent. I sometimes don't say what I am at all. I'm not being hypocritical; I don't want to be a hypocrite. The Roman Catholic Church people say to me then, 'But you're still a Roman Catholic.' And I say to them, 'well, I feel comfortable enough in a sense that I can go to church, and I like to go there too because I want to be with Him.' Do you understand where I'm comin' from with this?

"Ireland was Christianized. But Roman Catholicism destroyed them, and it destroyed the natural love of God that the Celts had. It was natural. It was there. They had a lovely feeling toward God. They did! They did! That's my belief of it. I mightn't be right, but that's what I feel. But I must say that I do feel comfortable with my God. Extremely fortunate. And I wish a lot of other people did too. Maybe that is part of the conflict in the world..."

"Could you say something about the Celtic Spirit?"

"With the Celtic spirit, it's the circle. The circle is the circle of life, no beginning, no end. The year... with the year, you have spring, you have summer, then you

297

have autumn, which is kind of the rainy season. Then you have winter, which is the end, but we're starting again. And that's what we get through in our weather in this country. We live for weather, and when you come to Ireland, as you will notice, everybody talks about the weather. That's goin' back to the Celtic nature. That's our spirit. We associate everything with the weather. And all the people out there in the garden, very much in touch with that. To me, it's very much like the Indians, the Native Americans, who were totally in tune with it. When we were visiting the States, I wanted to go somewhere I could feel that spirit. We went to the wrong reservation... We were in Canada, and we went to a reservation outside of Toronto. That kind of depressed me. We went in there. It was huge. You were actually in there before you realized it, and it was just a whole row of small houses. There were some impoverished people living there, and their spirit was gone. Crushed completely. What it made me think about was, gosh, it's the same thing. The Celts and the Native Americans. Quite similar, very similar. They worshipped God from inside. They weren't apart from God. They wanted to be part of Him. And everything to do with their rituals was associated with the earth—wind, fire, water, the air... the whole thing. We were the same. It saddened us so much. My son took it very badly. We were traumatized when we came out. We thought, gosh, this is bad. At least we've gone beyond that. The Famine came to mind. Another oppression again, eh? Similar thing again... someone else coming in and oppressing. And that happened to us in the Famine. It was very devastating to us because the land let us down. We developed a dependence on the earth, and a link between the earth and God. And how the people felt so desperate because God let them down, and the earth let them down. They trusted God and they trusted the earth, and they felt He let them down. Yet, they found Him again, because all they needed to see was somethin' growing. The devastation of the Famine was just horrible. But the Native Americans were one of the first people to actually help the Irish during the Famine. The Chocktaw Indians collected money and sent it over here. It just goes to show the affinity between the two nations.

"The spirit, the Celtic spirit... It's very difficult to explain because it's all linked to nature, is what it is. And God was there, but He didn't have a name. Because how could he have a name, when He was everything? OK, they had goddesses, and various spirit-gods and stuff like that. I was reading recently—was it John O'Donoghue's book? He said that the wake, the wake when someone died, actually was a Celtic ritual. The word 'pagan', of course, was always used; the word 'Celtic' was not learned. They never mentioned the word 'Celtic' in all the religion classes. Of course we never questioned that, obviously. But the word 'pagan'... everyone was a pagan. We were the one true religion. Pagans were nothing... But the pagans were our ancestors, and the pagans had it together better than the Roman Catholics. They had! They were in communion with God, naturally! And anyone could commune with God. And that's the Celtic spirit. That's what it's about... it's the earth.

"Then there were the faeries... not the Leprechauns. They came out at certain seasons—summer and the autumn. They were the times when the two worlds came close together, and that's what the Celts believed. There were two worlds, two planes, and you could cross over, depending on your gifts of spirituality. And if you were spiritual, you could actually cross over. There are countless stories of people who crossed over. It's fascinating. It really is! But if you go back to your roots, and read about it and study it, you see where it all comes from.

But religion can be abandoned, sadly to say. Religion isn't the be-all and end-all, it really isn't. It's an institution. It's a kind of institutionalized worship. We don't need that. We don't have to have it. It's in here... it's within. My favorite command is 'love your neighbor as yourself.' If you can't love yourself and love God, how can you love your neighbor? And another Celtic thing is the tribe, the community. We've lost that too. And the Celtic Tiger... people are becoming less community-oriented. The family is gone. The whole ritual of sitting down at the dinner table, without any television and the news, where you can sit, discuss the day, discuss anything you want... That actually is gone, almost gone. There aren't many of us left who actually do that. In a sense, belonging to somebody, to people, is gone... Maybe we're meant to get rid of religion and go back to our roots. Maybe there has to be a cleansing. Maybe in this next millennium, we'll be back to our origins..."

Someone walked in at that moment, so our conversation came to a natural close.

SOMETIMES A STAR...

the darkest time is just before the dawn...

Adrien was a man in his late fifties, maybe early six-ties. At first it was not clear if he really wanted to be talking with me or not, but once we got going, he seemed to be more comfortable. He seemed quite serious. Chimes were ringing out once again while we were sitting outside in the garden. The air was so sweet, and it was still. I asked Adrien where he found God, what sustained him..."

"I heard a man saying one day, 'I feel that God,' he

303

said, 'is very far away from me today.' And I said, 'Guess who has moved.' Daily Mass, daily communion, I believe, is the sustenance of my spiritual life. It's not always there, that we get daily Mass, but when I can, I always try to go. It really keeps me very close to the Lord. And I also feel very strongly in the power of the Sacrament of Confession. But I feel, unfortunately, that in our Church today, confession isn't as easily available as it always was. Maybe this is due to the work of the priests—the work they're doing, or maybe should be doing—that takes up their valuable time. For some people who would like to get confession during the week, it would not be available other than Saturday. And for somebody who would be away from the Lord in that time. The Holy Father himself has said he needs weekly confession. So if *he* needs weekly confession, what can we say for the rest of us?"

"Would it be available if you wanted it, if you asked for it?"

"Well, I would say that if you went to a priest's house and you knocked on his door and said, 'Could I make confession,' that wouldn't be a problem. But I think that the sacrament is such a strong sacrament that it would be marvelous if we did have a priest available, let's say every day, so people could go to confession, if they'd want to go to confession. I don't mean the same person would be goin' to confession every day, but for people to know that the Sacrament of repentance is there, available, every day, plus Saturday. We would have confession on the first Fridays normally, and that appears to be something that has slipped away as well. We don't have confessions on the first Thursday anymore, either. So, in my spiritual life, it would be the Sacrament of the Eucharist and the Sacrament of Confession. Especially the Eucharist, especially that... the Lord is always with us. The best way I can describe it, I feel, 'twould be like a switch in the wall, bringing the electricity into our home. Christ is always present within us, but it's only we that can turn on that switch. We've the power to turn it on, and to turn it off. The bulb might be in the ceiling all the time, but it may not be lighting. But the power is going to the bulb... and so to us. We have the power to flip that switch on and off. We can switch the switch off in our daily life with the Lord, or we can switch it on. He leaves that decision with us. How do ya feel, what do you think of that?

Make sense?"

"What I find often when I encourage people, and remind myself as well, is that we always have choices. I believe it's in Deuteronomy, where it says, 'I set before you life and death, blessing and curse... choose life!' At any given moment in any day, if we just step back and look at whatever we're doing or thinking, or making a decision or whatever... we're choosing what's life-giving, or not. Y'know, a lot of people are angry. They're consumed by their anger. If they only realize that they are really choosing that. We could also choose peace, at any given moment, or choose Christ. It's the kind of stuff, it sounds almost simplistic... It's the kind of stuff that transformation is made of. It can change your life."

"What concerns me greatly is the lack of respect that is creeping into the Catholic Church. There is a lot of disrespect taking place within the Church. If somebody doesn't say, 'stop' shortly, we won't have any respect left. We must accept that Christ's house is His palace. And if we go into a palace, we have to have respect for the king. And when we go into a church, especially the church here, where the Blessed Sacrament is exposed, we have to have respect. And that is something that is slipping within our church. It's a grave concern to me, really. And I would say maybe not done intentionally by people, unintentionally in certain circumstances. But it's a bad example, then, to younger people as well, y'know. So, to get back to the sustenance of life... I certainly would believe that the Eucharist is what we have to live on. If I found myself away from the Lord, or distant from the Lord in any way. I'd find it hard to describe. But I would find... a kind of emptiness, something I couldn't touch. So, back to the Sacrament, up to confession and the Blessed Eucharist, where I can really feel quite close to the Lord.

"I organize lots of trips. I have been organizing many trips since 1984 to Medjugorje and Yugoslavia. I went there myself in 1984. It wasn't an organized trip. I went, I s'pose, really out of curiosity. Like many people were saying these happenings were taking place. I was like a doubting Thomas, and I went to see for myself. When I went there, what I saw was the faith of thousands of people—not in the alleged visions of Our Lady that were taking place there—but thousands of people that attended Mass each day and queued in the fields for confession. It was a sight to behold; to see maybe two hundred people queued up to a priest. Two hundred people to a priest. Having been to Medjugorje on many occasions and all the alleged visions that are happenin' nowadays, people would ask me, 'Did you see something there? What did you see? You must have seen something.' I didn't. But I did see the transformation of people, and their respect, and their love of the Lord in the Blessed Sacrament. And especially the people themselves, the looks on their faces during the Mass, especially at the Consecration of the Mass, and especially young people. To see most people on their knees with their hands elevated to the Lord, in total respect. 'Twas a sight to behold. So that's where I center my spiritual life. Whether that's any help to you or not…"

"Oh, yes, very much. Some are saying that this is a time of darkness for the Church right now, not just Ireland, everywhere. What I find helps me is to keep in mind that the darkest time of the night is just before the dawn. And that even though people are discouraged and wondering why aren't the young people going to Church anymore, and where is their faith, it's important to remember that they may not be going into the front doors of the church, but maybe Christ is still very alive for

them, in them..."

"Well, as you said, Sister, the darkest time is just before the dawn. Certainly this morning, the darkness was just before the dawn, when I got up at 4 o'clock. This morning is the morning I usually do the Adoration of the Blessed Sacrament, from 5 to 6. And to go there every Monday morning, and to be present with the Lord for that particular hour is a great grace in my life. And to take over from the person who goes before me, and for the person who follows me. For those people to be coming, in prayer, and at an early hour of the morning, it shows that there are many benefits—graces given—for their homes, for their families. And I think for the bishop here, especially in our diocese, to have brought Eucharistic Adoration into the diocese, for the convent here and at the cathedral, it's had many blessings in our town. And I think that has kind of borne fruit. Like even yesterday, the bishop informed us after Mass, yesterday morning, that he has ten young boys lined up for the priesthood again this coming year. Whereas in many of the dioceses around the country, they haven't got any young people going for the priesthood. But, for sure, it's the power of prayer, the power of the Adoration. The priesthood and vocations for the priesthood is stronger here than anywhere else. I think that the Lord is listening to our prayers.

"I think people may not realize the full extent, the true Presence of Christ, in the Blessed Sacrament. I think that if we were to walk around the corner now, and go into the church, and to see Christ present at the altar with His red robe and black flowing beard as we see Him in the pictures and photographs on the wall... I'm sure if we saw Him, we would be taken aback a great deal and we would fall on our knees before Him. I firmly believe that Christ is truly present in the Blessed Sacrament in the church right now, and in every church in the world. But especially where Adoration of the Blessed Sacrament is exposed. And I think that if people truly believed that Christ's presence was there, they would spend a lot more time before the Blessed Sacrament in prayer. Rather than, maybe, lying on the beach, or going shopping, or going to a football match or something like that. But I think it's in the area where we have to grow, where we have to grow a great deal. And maybe for many of us it will take all our lives, to come to that point... to realize God's True Presence, the closeness, the True Presence..."

well, Sister, we don't get involved with things like that...

Fran was a woman in her late forties, maybe early fifties, dressed not unlike a gypsy, wearing a brightly colored scarf around her head. She appeared quite animated, very energetic. We agreed to meet at Shannon Airport. We sat outside in a little garden area, and needless to say, it was somewhat disconcerting whenever a plane took off and I had to ask her to please repeat what she said several times! But we persevered...

311

"A few years ago, our parish priest always asked me, 'Right, Fran, you've got a bird's eye view, count the heads in the church.' So I would count the congregation downstairs, and it might come to something like a hundred and sixty five to a hundred and eighty. And recently I've been counting, and my choir, which was made up of twenty-eight children, is now five children. And the congregation... I'm counting thirty-two. Numbers have definitely dropped. Also, the numbers in the priesthood have dropped as well. Some of our parishes are finding it hard to get a priest for the late-night Mass. So we're down to two priests, in our parish. We had three. They're now talking about combining our parish with Shannon, which would probably give us access to more priests. But at the same time there is a fall-out."

"What do you attribute it to? What are people saying, why is this happening?"

"I suppose... well, some people will say, 'oh, 'tis all because of Bishop Casey, and what Bishop Casey did, and Annie Murphy.' They had a lot to do with it. They lost faith in the church, with bishops falling. And some other bishop, I think he was an African, did the same thing. And they attribute it a lot to, well... I s'pose, the priests are a bit more into the worldly side of things today. You see them all out there, getting involved in the pub, having their drink, and some of the younger lads going to the dances, and things like that. For some reason or other, I feel none of us has the right to judge any of them, no matter what they do. That is their own business, and I won't be accountable for any one of them. So I have no notion of losing my faith or not going to church, or anything else, to accommodate anyone else who is doing that. Y'know, I don't feel I have the right to judge. Would you agree?"

"Yes."

"'Tis sad, because I've seen a lot of young clergymen come in, and they try so hard when they come to our parish. Then within months you see the strain on their faces, and then you lose a lovely young priest. One of our young curates, he left. He was finding it just so hard. But I think people as well were making it difficult for him. He didn't get a chance. I would say, in our parish, the young man did not get a chance, you know, with the women. That kind of thing. He was a lovely,

313

handsome young man. Part of his downfall, I s'pose...
But he left the church. I had always felt that his Mass
was beautiful. I mean, when it came to the consecration
of the Mass, I just looked up at the altar and it felt so
good because he said Mass so beautifully. He didn't do
an up-down with the Host and say, 'Body of Christ'
kind-of-a thing. When he held the Host up you saw the
pain in his face, the way he looked at it, and he just kept
it up there for the people to venerate. And the same with
the Chalice. And I thought that was so lovely... beautiful. And I find, too, that one thing that annoys me in
church is the way we run through the prayers, and the
'Our Father' is said with such disrespect, really, because
we just lither-blither and get through it. My husband is
Church of Ireland and I go with him as well. I take the
Sunday school there and I do the readings in his church.
And I do the readings and take the choir in my own.
When I go down there, I listen to the way they say the
'Our Father,' all line by line, with such sincerity, and
they really mean it when they say it. I love the 'Our
Father' because it is the only prayer that our Lord left us,
y'know. So to me, that would be my most important
prayer. And after that, then, are all my own personal
prayers, which is mostly 'chit-chat.' But the 'Our

Father,' I love the way the Protestants say it. I just feel that I would love to slow down the people in my church, make them pray, and maybe keep quiet before Mass as well. That's another thing... all the talk that goes on before when we should really be preparing for what's coming. Just little things like that that I feel could help us. To me they are very important... we should prepare before Mass, attend Mass, and do the chit-chat afterwards."

(A brief pause, then she continued.)

"Numbers are dropping off, and 'tis sad. But then I read my Missionary book, and I look at it and the pages are filled with young clergy abroad in foreign countries that are all going for the Church. And you see forty new young clerics ordained, and you'd think that maybe someday they'll come back to Ireland, and get that little spark goin' again in Ireland. That's been said now... We have a lot of good people in my parish. Y'know, I wouldn't leave my parish. I love my parish, and I love the people that are there. They're good, but I feel they just need that little push back to reality, push back to what it all was and what it really means. Bring them back to...

bring them back to prayer and the Mass as it should be, and back to what it's supposed to be. They're becoming lax.

"I feel we're very much gone into materialism as well. That has an awful lot to do with it. There are many things out there on the social scene, and the church is really when you have the time. I find with my own teenagers, it's hard to get them to go to church. My husband has one of them in his church. He put her playing the tapes. He said, 'Well, that'll keep her there.' I feel if you can give them a job, y'know. The children in my choir now, there are only five... Our sacristan died recently, so I decided to get on to the Canon, and he agreed that we could take over the cleaning of the church and the cleaning of the flowerbeds. So I rounded them up the other day at the altar and gave them their rakes and shovels and rubber gloves and what have you, and we spent two hours doing flowerbeds. They *loved* it! So I feel that really at a very early age, children want to be involved. You cannot get the adults to get up to the altar and do a reading. And at first Canon didn't want the children up, but last Sunday I went to him and caught him— we got in through the back door, like a hurling team— caught him when he was down!" *(a little laugh)* "And he said, 'Look, I'm trying to get the readers for my church from inside in the village, and I can't get them to do it. If you are able to get even children to go up to that altar, then up with them!' He did say no one could go on the altar and read unless they were fourteen. But now I've got the little ones up. Like I say, 'tis wonderful. But I think the reality is starting to dawn on him, that if you don't get them when they're young, and get them involved, you're not going to get them when they're teenagers. They're too shy to go up then. But I find now, I have the little ones and get them to the altar. It means the parents have to read the Gospel or read the lesson with them and go over it with them And I'm telling the parents to make sure their diction is good and that they take their time, and that they read as if they mean it. And remember, when they say the last line at the end of that lesson, 'This is the Word of the Lord,' it's not the word of Charlie Hall here, one of our politicians. It's the Word of the Lord! Therefore, you make sure that everyone gets it. Right? So, then you have the parents involved. And I feel that's important because the whole family is dragged into it, to make sure that the little darlin' does good on the altar." (*Short laugh.*) "I don't know what you think. But that's it…"

317

"Oh, no, it doesn't matter really what I think. I'm just listening and trying to draw out people's different experiences. I would like to ask you something, I don't know if you are prepared to answer, but Pat told me a little bit about your life, and that for a while you were a Sister?"

"Oh, I was…with the Sisters of Mercy, up in New Zealand. Loved every minute of it. But my sister was getting married at the time, and she didn't want to leave my parents. They were both old, and she was feelin' very guilty, being the last one at home. We had only three girls in the family. So I thought, well, sure I could go home, and re-enter at home… 'Mercies' all over the world, y'know… 'tis one message you're bringing. Anyway, I left and came home with the intentions of re-entering again. So I said I would see how my parents were. If you were at the other side of the world, and you have a sister writing a letter to you and feeding you all this sob story, you don't *really* know how things are at home. When I came home, I discovered that my parents were literally not as bad as she had thought, because she was with them all the time. They were bouncin' around! So, I thought of entering the Poor Clares, who were

318

nearby. For some reason or another, I went to the Poor Clares, because they were in Ennis then. My mother was always talking about them and the great work they do and their prayer and all this. So I just said I'd go over and re-enter. And there was a notice up on the door, 'Sisters on retreat from the 28th of July to the 28th of August,' their long retreat. I said, that's grand, I'll wait. In the meantime, I took a job working at the airport. And my future husband came to work there as well. He asked me out, so I said sure, I might as well go out and kill time. And I went out with him, we went to a film, and then to one the following week. We just seemed to drift into a happy relationship, and we kind of knew straight away that we wanted to get married without anyone talkin' about it. So, that's how I ended up in marriage.

"But I do feel that with what I am doing today as a lay person is probably more than if I had stayed in the convent. When I was in the convent, I saw a poor woman across the road with nine children, lying on a bed, deeply depressed, and a husband who was totally useless. I always wanted to go up and help that woman because I had her children in my class. And I mentioned it to the Superior and I was told, 'Well, Sister, we don't get involved in things like that. You have a job, you live

by the rules.' Then we went to visit hostels, and we went
to visit the mental hospital, and I saw a lot of distressed
people and a lot of parents coming in with stress on their
faces. But it was always the case that we didn't get
involved. So I just felt that when I came home, I was free
to do that. Like, my job in the convent was really to get
up in the morning, say my prayers, meditate, go to Mass.
Had a beautiful room, had everything I wanted, the best
of food, the best of everything. There was no scarcity of
anything. In actual fact, 'twas the life of luxury. Right?
It was luxurious, compared to the people who lived all
around our convent. We were up on a mountain and we
were living in a mansion. But I was looking out on a
ghetto. For miles all these timber huts, and all these little children coming into school badly clad and all this. I
realized there was an awful lot of poor in the world, and
I always kind of felt that we should be out there doing
something. We should be out there among those people. Y'know, there were barriers there that we could have
taken down. Maybe fear had a lot to do with it. But I am
afraid of no one... When I left the convent, for a while I
took the job at the airport, and then I got married. And
then I started to say, well now, there's more to this than
just getting his dinner! So I decided to get involved in a

few things... So for the last ten or eleven years, I'm working with the gypsies, the traveling community, and the poor of my parish whenever I see the need, y'know? Because it doesn't just stop with gypsies...

"I look at the town of Ennis where I came from. It used to be a grand town, with all the little shops and all the little streets and people running small businesses. But at least they were out there in their door with their vegetables, outside their doors. And they knew everyone. It was a great social thing for them, running these little businesses. I went there a couple of years back. I had a great experience, and got a great insight into it, because I was looking at Ennis from a different point of view. I thought it was a brilliant town, a new technological town, winning all the awards and the councilors patting themselves on the back. And then I went down the road to start a studio, open a studio with a few others, overhead a little shop down on Parnell Street. So when we went about it to get insurance, we were told, 'Oh, the fire department has to be brought in, and they'll have to pass it,' y'know, to make sure that it was safe. So when the fire department came in, they closed the little shop down. The man lost his business... and we lost our studio. So they're declaring all the old businesses down along Parnell Street and all the other small streets... they're declaring them fire hazards. And when they're declared as a fire hazard, they automatically have to close down or find the money to do them up and make them safe. Business after business is being closed down.

"You could roughly say in my town, Ennis, six men practically own the whole town. They're big developers. And every road out of Ennis—you've got five roads leading out of Ennis—I would say for up to two and a half to three miles out of the town, on every road, you have private developments owned by the very, very rich people. And there is no green land left in or around town to build for the poor.

"So the poor will be eased out of town, and the big men will have their businesses in town. And the poor and the gypsies, the travelers, they will all end up three miles out. And these are the people that don't always have the transport or always have the money. So, I'm kind of cross with my local county council. I'm up and down to see them all the time and I'm up and down to Dublin to talk to the Ministers. I just feel that... y'know, it's a showpiece. They have spent a fortune patting themselves on the back for doing all of this. And the teenagers are spending as if there were no tomorrow. Y'know, it's money, money, money...

"It costs sixty thousand to build a halting site for travelers. The halting site would consist of four wash-rooms and four high concrete walls so they would have basic facilities. And the Council said, 'We haven't got the money.' Fifty thousand it's costing us to build a halt-ing site. But they built a road into Limerick and put a bridge going into the town nearby, an up and over bridge. And I believe that they had a day in one of the hotels, to pat themselves on the back again for building a bit of a road. I got to know a girl who worked with the hotel. And the girl at the desk told me when I mentioned to her that it cost fifty thousand to build a halting site, she said, 'Well, it cost more than the price of two halting sites for the one day's drinking and eating that went on in our hotel.' Right? So... that's the kind of local gov-ernment we have up in Ennis.

"We have a temporary halting site in Ennis. It was built as a temporary site, but in the future they're not building any more of these. They're actually goin' to build residential sites, which means that the traveling families will be in there and it will belong to them. Whereas we have these halting sites where a crowd can come in, halt, then move on... find another halting site.

323

They couldn't even do that for these people. So this is the kind of thing I will be fighting for with the travelers."

"You sound very busy, very active, and very dedicated. I ask the question, what sustains you?"

"I see Christ in every one of them. That's what keeps me going. I'm not doing it just for the love of doing volunteer work or social work. But I really see Christ in the underprivileged and the poor. I know that the extremely rich need Him too, right? But I still see Him more in the poor and the underprivileged. That is what keeps me going."

"What do you see for the future of the Church?"

"I believe that the future of the Church will be very, very strong. 'T'will probably be smaller in number, but then I feel that it is quality that counts, not quantity, y'know? So the people who are there will be good... The good people in my community, they will always pass on what they've got onto their children. They're very, very good. I hear about all this badness and corruption that's out there... like the people in Shannon say the

324

travelers in Shannon are the most violent people on the road. They're kind of aggressive, all right, but, they're very good people. You see, many of them are mentally ill. Mental illness is really right throughout all the travelers, across the length and breadth of Ireland. It's just because they're exposed to dreadful conditions, and your environment makes you what you are. They haven't access to anything that we have; they haven't got an easy life. Fourteen people all bunched together in a small little room. The space for mobility within the little caravan may only be the size of my kitchen table. Right? And you're talking about kids crawling over couches to get down to another place, and all this kind of thing. They've no space. Lack of space causes aggression. I feel that space is their major problem. They've never been given a caravan to go with the size of their family. Maybe fifteen hundred Euros were spent on every home of the travelers. And after that, if they want anything bigger, they have to try to beg on the streets or make money any way they can to try to find a bigger one for themselves. And they still won't own it, because the council put down the first fifteen hundred. They own it, the council. It's in their name. And that of course is very frustratin' for a traveler not spending more money on looking for a bigger caravan, 'cause they won't own it. Right? But lack of space, to me, is causing massive aggression, and therefore I feel that there is a very high rate of mental illness throughout all the nomads in Ireland. 'Cause I've seen the ones that have been given the space. I've seen those who have been housed up in Ennis. And I watched the transition. I watched them all calm down. I've seen it. It is unbelievable. The kids are sleeping better, they're looking cleaner, they settle better in the schools. The ones I work with are the ones on the side of the road, and I see how aggressive they are compared to the ones in houses. And I see the conditions they live in and how grubby and dirty their poor children are. And then I see them get a house and you see the transformation. Just unbelievable, absolutely unbelievable... The parents change, the children change... they are more receptive to learning. They go into the schools and they are more rested. They are more able to relate.

"Some of the children now, they're still at the side of the road, they've gone into the secondary school in Shannon. They're marvelous! I go in and sit down and I chat with them. But it's very hard for them. They haven't got the facilities, they haven't got electricity there. Especially the winter nights, after 4 o'clock it's startin' to get dark and you'll see the little ones screwing up their eyes trying to read the books and do their home-work. They get out from school at half-three or quarter to four and by half-four 'tis dark. Y'know? They have no running water. They've no bathroom facilities. And the local farmers will complain that they are using their fields. Where do you want them to go now? What do you do with them? Haven't got the facilities... The local council will not give the facilities, and they're getting all these little committees going for talk and consultative committees and what have you. The county council, you see, will form a committee very quickly when they want to have a stalling tactic. So let's form a committee and talk about it, and this would go on for eighteen months. They did that a few years ago. Right... now the outcome of this means half a dozen men to redefine what we have said for another committee to form. So they're talking again now for another year, right? They haven't given up the plans drawn up for the six sites that are comin' up to Ennis because they're putting roundabouts and new motorways through the town. But as yet they haven't decided where the roads will come through, so until that is all finished, they cannot start planning for the travel-ers. That would have to be put off again for another five years, and they're living in filth and squalor…

"So we're fighting this at the moment. I went on the air there for an hour two weeks ago, and have been on pleading for a family all week, looking for funding because their caravan burned down. The council gave fifteen hundred, and they were cross about me going on the air. And I thought, 'Goody,' 'cause that is why I went on the air! I wanted to get an opportunity to let all the county know that if they only gave fifteen hundred, fifteen hundred wouldn't put in windows in anyone's house. So why do they expect to put a roof on a full house over twelve people's heads? I wanted to get that opportunity from time to time… I calm down for a little while, but then all of a sudden I'll flare up again. I'm a bit like the devil then, I think!" *(Laughter.)* "People sit around waiting to see when will she rise again! But y'know, you have to… If the council would do something good, I would give them a slight pat on the back. Y'know, give praise where praise is due. Not too often, it doesn't happen too often, but if they do something that's good, we'll recognize that. We don't want to bad-mouth or run down anyone. We're not doing it for the sake of *doing* it. I don't like doing it. I get no pleasure out of it. But I mean, when you see wrong happening in your community, it doesn't matter who it happens to, you have to challenge it. I think challenge is a very good thing."

"Thanks so much. And good luck to you!"

SOMETIMES A STAR...

a most deafening peace I've ever known...

John was around twenty years of age when we met. He was a budding journalist.

We sat on a grassy slope, overlooking the town. The cathedral was nearby.

"You just want to get really what I think Ireland is like, and the whole Celtic thing..."

"Your thoughts and feelings about, yes, the Celtic thing, the Celtic Spirit. Countless authors are writing about this subject, both here in Europe and over in the

331

States. Books and books are being written that are often based on the past. I couldn't help wonder what people are thinking and feeling today. I am finding there are a lot of very strong feelings about the church, good and bad. Apparently many aren't going to Church. I want to get a spectrum, different perspectives, especially different ages. But I also want people to feel free and comfortable, that if they're not going to church, could they say why. And if they're not going—like yourself—where are you being sustained, what's life-giving for you in your life?"

"Do ya need spirituality as well, is that what you're lookin' for?"

"Whatever it is that keeps you going. That's really what I'm looking for. And if you have some of your own kind of spirituality that you want to share, that's important... If this is going to be a book, I hope it's going to be available in Ireland, not just for American readers. I spoke with a Sister of Mercy before, and I asked her, 'If you have any words of encouragement, can you say them?' And she did. And I think it was very worthwhile. She herself said, 'Yeah, people aren't going to church,

but it doesn't mean they don't have a spirituality or a faith.' So that's the kind of thing I want to hear. Whatever it is that sustains you... you might go to the mountains or whatever. Just because you're not going to church doesn't mean you don't have a faith."

"Well, I s'pose, really, I think the reason why the Catholic Church went down in Ireland is because it's a bit more educated country now, and we also have seen what other countries have seen. We only picked up really in the last maybe thirty years. The poverty thing was an everyday lifestyle in Ireland up to, I'd say, the '70s, when people started goin' on holidays and not be thinking when is their son goin' to emigrate and all the rest of it. That can be a cliché at times, but it was actually realistic, y'know? If you go around this town, everybody knows an emigrant. So it isn't a cliché, really... it's there, like. In 1845, obviously, was our historic Famine. And there were those who were protecting the nation, and were tellin' then the people who only wanted to hear what they felt about it, and it kind of backfired on them. And then in the 1970', we were getting better educated. But you only learned what they wanted you to learn. 'Twas a shame."

I asked John when he realized he wasn't interested in going to church.

"It would have been, if I had my way, it would have been at10, I'd say, or even earlier. Why... kids are always bored, y'know. You have to do this, you have to do that. And I'm not someone who follows rules, y'know, 'to have to...' And I'm not interested in organized religion, anyway, in any shape, size or form. It's what you believe yourself... Religion is within. Spirituality is from within. In other words, that means because human beings are free, then we shouldn't be settin' rules in how you should practice your faith or whatever. Obviously, some rules are made for a reason. You don't drive on the wrong side of the road because it would cause a crash. But you don't need that in religion, because religion should be our own interpretation. And spirituality as well. And it's just as much the same with the Celtic thing. They had rules, certainly, but there were a different set of 'em. But nowadays, we are well educated, most everybody goes to college. We've caught up with America and other countries now, because everybody wants to go to college. There are very few people now who go and do a trade. I s'pose it's a shame in oth-

334

er ways. But it's showing that we're moving on, developing further. Trades aren't as important now as they were, y'know. And you have people, like myself, who would be saying 'what the hell are we doing,' the usual questions that you ask. That's a part of everyday culture now, rather than having maybe just one or two, maybe 10, eleven pretentious Bohemian writers in a corner, writin' poems about it, y'know. Which I don't have a problem with, of course. But I think students are asking the questions. When I say students, the movers and the shakers, y'know, like it's always been. Paris in the '60s, people like that. They got it movin', they changed the world.

(John paused a moment, reflectively...) "I just have a problem with the whole magnificence of it all, y'know? I'm probably wrong, but I think that it should be simple, I mean, like it is now, sittin' out here on this grass. The Natural Being is the more important thing than the granite monstrosity that's over there. OK, maybe some people need it, but I don't think ya do."

"So even though you don't go to church, you're still aware of God's presence?"

335

"Oh yeah, absolutely…"

"Where? Where do you find it?"

"Well, it's a very difficult question to answer. I probably would have been able to answer that better a few years ago, but now it's different, I think. Y'see, my whole sorta theory on it is the whole Darwin thing, you know of course, it evolves. But y'see, there had to have been a catalyst, a starting of it going. So I'll say, when the Big Bang happened, right? And who or what was behind that Big Bang? It was obviously the Creator. And all this now is just a follow-on from that. But there had to be something to get it started. My whole theory on it is that, He said, 'Look, here's the world, go on and see what you can do with it now. And I'll come back to ya later on and we'll have a chat'."

"Hmmm… Where were you a few years ago?"

"Spiritually, you say?"

"Yes…"

"Oh, I probably would have been at the mountains and the sea and all the rest of it, y'know. But I got evolved. It evolves with everyone. I would never stay stagnant in one stage at all. I never have. I would find it difficult to stay in one place because, because you continue to eradicate ideas, and you make new ones. You learn something else from them. It's a continuous learning. A learning curve that never stops, really..."

"Do you still go to the sea and the mountains? Do you still find a degree of solace there?"

"Oh, yeah... What it really is that it's just a good feeling, really, you know you can't describe it. It's like, uh, I think it's the most, the most relaxing thing, the sea. The sea is gorgeous. Obviously, if you've been up to the mountains before, and you've felt what it's like to be up there. A most deafening peace that I've ever known..."

"And do you still look for that, then?"

"Oh, yeah... actively seek it out."

The soft sound of the nearby stream could be heard,

337

the water rippling gently down the hill.

"I would say there is a plan for everybody. It's like another cliché, but it's actually true, like. Now if you look at the North, right? Northern Ireland... If they were obsessed with the spirituality of it rather than the mood-dominated lunacy, we wouldn't have had what we had for so many years. They're bound to keep the tradition. If they had kept on moving on and thinking with new ideas rather than thinking about the old, maybe they wouldn't be marchin' down the road... or killin' each other. Absolute lunacy. But then, that's the Irish thing, because they would have destroyed everyone in the sense of the Celtic thing. They lose out, and no matter whether you were Protestant or Catholic or Buddhist, if you're Irish, you're still seeking for the thing you lost. It's the psyche..."

The two of us sat there quietly for a few minutes, listening to the stream, taking in the present moment...

"I think regardless of what age any of us is, my take on it is that there is a longing in all of us. What we do with it is a very personal thing and very individualistic.

Some of the older folk that I've been talking with, they're very much into the traditional. I have a nephew who is into Joseph Campbell and Huston Smith. He is very open. Doesn't go to church, but he is definitely a thinker and a seeker. I see that as quite common in the younger generation, whether in the States or here."

"It has to do with the education, again, I presume, really... the more you can learn what you want to learn, rather than having to learn about what they want you to learn. I remember, it was ridiculous... In school you were told that this or that is the thing you have to say when you go to confession. This I find difficult, this whole stringent reality that they follow, y'know? I think that the whole thing is so unbelievable that it must be surreal. You must think of it surreally... that you must go to a priest in a box, venerate, and say, 'I'm sorry.' Then they go along and they say later that it's all the big picture, the whole thing, the grass or whatever else is your religion. They completely contradict themselves later. Because if that was the case, you wouldn't need a, what's the word, a conduit, is it? ...to say you're sorry..."

"Why couldn't you go directly to..."

"...to the grass, or to the stones, or whatever... It seems ridiculous to me, seems a contradiction." *(Pause.)* "But you're dead right, because the whole searching and the longing thing is within everybody, you just don't have to be Irish, of course. But I think, your own nation... it lost its identity as well, in that sense. And I don't mean this in a derogatory sense, because literally we were deemed the bastard race. Others came in and removed what was originally there, and set up for themselves. Many Irish people believe that. I have no problem with the United States, but I think it was a shame that they lost what their own original spirituality was, the Native Americans.

"When we were in Canada, we visited the Seven Nations reservation. It was a shock to all of us... just the way they were treated. It was fascinating. They were treated like second-class citizens. When we asked people about them, outside of Hamilton, which was just down the road, they just wouldn't talk about 'em. They laughed and they joked. It was all this deep-embedded racism, y'know, about how these people are less because they're country people and they're obsessed with land. I

340

don't know... that's what I saw. I spent an hour talkin' to a cousin of mine. I never thought I'd meet someone who was so racist about the whole thing. 'Cause when we visited them, we had utter respect for 'em. I don't know, maybe they're troublemakers. It's the same as the travelers in Ireland. The itinerants, as they're called. They're people who have their own culture, but unfortunately through misadventure, they decide to go into bars and wreck the place. But then, they're all tarred with the same brush, and there might be only five or six in each clan that would cause trouble. But that's the same with the Native Americans as well as in Ireland. The same the world over. Everybody's the same.

"I was talking to an American girl in college. She was studying archeology. She showed me a picture of arrowheads that they found near her home, and they were ordinary Native American arrowheads. The Celtic arrowheads are exactly the same. So I said to her, 'It's amazing that people like my people were over there' And she thought I was crazy, completely. Oh, I don't know, maybe I was. But that's the problem with religion as well. You're taught not to respect everyone's beliefs. Like if you're Protestant, you're not supposed to have communion in a Catholic church, or have communion in a Protestant church if you're a Catholic. Like our President said she was going to have communion at a funeral Mass in a Protestant church, and she was berated from the highest. It's a shame, right?"

"Mm hmm... but I'm sure she knew what she was doing..."

"Oh, it was a statement, yeah. Absolutely."

"We need more people like that. We need more people who have the courage to take a stand, and to live out of that, that, 'within' place. And I think it may be happening. Part of it is just giving people the opportunity to speak their minds, to say what it is that they really believe in..."

"Well, what I think is intriguing, though... You know, some people, in one of our political parties, they think that the devil is within the flesh. I can't figure it that way at all. Because the thing is, I don't know... I just find it difficult, some of their agendas, y'know... but that's slightly disturbing, I think, with the whole dysfunctional view of religion."

"When we use terms like 'the press' or 'the Church,' these are made of individuals. So you might have some individuals who certainly have quite a bit of the devil in them, in the press as well as the Church! But likewise, you'll find just as many individuals, hopefully a lot more, who have a lot of God in them. But when we start making generalizations, that's when we go wrong. We have to remember that when we make generalizations like that, it's often out of fear."

"I think we're all prone to generalizations because it's in our nature. I think the difficulty with the individual thing is that we never stop thinking, in respect to that. But then some, by their nature, they must have control. The whole control freak thing... I'm not an anarchist at all, but I really believe that people should make their own decisions. So maybe I shouldn't be actively seeking spirituality in that sense, because there are supposed to be rules attached to it, y'know? Oh, I don't know, maybe I got off the point..."

"Well, the spirituality of that 'within place' you mentioned before is very deep. And there aren't any rules attached to that. We could be seeking God's

343

Presence in any given moment in the day... in the clouds, in the water, in the gentle sound of the little stream right here. No rules attached..."

"Not at all, no. You just sit there and you listen."

"You've got it. And if you can be open to it, be replenished..."

"Yeah..." *(A hesitation.)* "Would you say now since you came here... Sorry for asking a question, but... that you've seen a confusion within everybody, in Ireland especially, because of the way the situation is at the moment?"

"Not so much confusion as anger. There seems to be some anger, especially with a few of the ones in the older generation. And I sense some fear. Some want to cling; they want to cling as long as they can to the old traditions. They don't want to see change. They're very quick to judge the young people who are leaving the Church. And yet, others of that generation seem to be more... well, they ponder more. They seem to be more thoughtful, even though they still are, I would say, tradi-

tionalists. But they seem to also have a touch of grace. Maybe it's healthy... Maybe some of these signs are healthy."

"Mmmm. I would say that I'm quite, um, in regards to confrontation, prone to it. But I don't know where that comes from. As an individual, being confrontational would probably be in the genes. Like, young people get into all kinds of confrontations, for whatever reasons..."

"Oh, they sure do! I was your age once. You don't have to be young, either. Is it a matter of being young? Perhaps it's in one's nature. I too... I mean the age that I am, which isn't that old (!), I know I've been a thorn in people's sides. Isn't it somebody's nature to ask questions, to question what is? What is it, really? Isn't what we're talking about here simply being a seeker of the truth? We both share that—we have that trait in common! I too can sometimes be confrontational, because there is something in me, very, very deep, that is always seeking and looking for the truth."

"It's back to the education thing again. You've obviously been educated, highly educated, right? And you actively sought the education to understand what it is, right?"

"Maybe... psychology, philosophy, human develop-ment... all that."

"You're far more educated than I would ever be. Maybe I will finally finish college someday..."

"You're young!"

"Y'know, but I am actively seeking that as well. You go to every college and you're goin' to have... well, the Socialist Party is in every college. Hundreds of con-frontational young people join it every year. And all they're looking for really is to protest, y'know? And I think the more educated you are, the more you question, and thus, the more confrontational you become because you have to question, eh? And you're not getting any answers, so naturally, fists go up... I mean fists within the mind, actually. Back to Paris yet again, right? You look at the way Paris was. That was complete anarchy, but that was because the educated people stood up. And Tiananmen Square. Right? It was peaceful. But because the autorities feared the education of the people who were questioning them, they attacked them. I think that spirituality exists in things like that. And it's seeing the human race at its very most vulnerable, and at its most impressive. Because let's face it, the ants in the ground are wonderful, but they haven't built what we have, y'know? And I think there are side effects to it that we destroyed. Like this would have been our woodland, thousands of years ago, before the Celts came, and the Phoenicians. But now it's this ruled, governed path and grass. I think it's a shame, but then again maybe it's a good thing because you wouldn't have this beautiful building now behind us, right? That is absolutely wonderful lookin', eh? No matter what way you look at it. And maybe the monstrosity is good-lookin' as well..." *(The nearby cathedral.)* "It's architecturally wonderful, but... It's foreboding, if you look at it. It's like a temple of spikes. It's my opinion, sorry..."

"Oh, it's all right... Anger is a form of passion in disguise. We speak of Christ and His Passion, and for many, Christ is our model. Very often we have to go through stages of anger, and it's OK, because hopefully it will lead to a sense of healing, and wholeness. We

347

hope that's where we are all heading, whatever age we are. Maybe it's the nature of the beast, being human, to question. And when one questions, one can't help but bump into walls. Almost the natural outcome of this is to be angry. Who wants walls? Once again, our nature, I think, is to try to see the walls crumble. But I do believe that God is inviting us to go deeper, and beckoning all of us, to ask questions. Whatever God is for each of us; a Transcendent Being, a sense of the all Good, Love or Peace, whatever it is that most of us is longing for...God is always beckoning. The Christ I know, the God I know, certainly isn't standing there with a big stick or hitting you over the head..."

"Oh, absolutely, yeah..."

"And so the Church maybe has done a lot of injustices to all of us, not just to those of you here in Ireland."

"Y'know, there's a part in me that wants to build a dam, so maybe it's a sort of control thing. Y'see, contradictions, yet again! But if you see it, I mean, kids... all they want to do is build dams in rivers. I mean, you probably did it yourself. Y'know, where you get a few stones and a bit of mortar, whatever, and you think you're a star if you dam up the river. And it's then the power of it when you remove the stone, you see it flowin'. That's the education, then, you see. You could use that as a metaphor. I think that's what you see with young peo- ple..." *(Another pause.)* "Gardening is like a subcon- scious act of control."

"Cultivating a garden, yes... manicuring the gar- den. But there's another side to that. Saying its control is one perspective, one way of seeing it. Another is a sense of order. Some people like to have a sense of order around them. Other people like it sort of 'au naturel'... let it just grow naturally."

"Yeah, but that's not conducive to easy living, y'know? Now, if I was at my garden, it might be an eco- logical study for the outback, y'know! I'm sure that I'd be arrested or something, because people would be quib- bling..." *(He smiled.)* "Did you ever see the movie 'The Matrix'? I think it's very spiritual. Very, very good. I enjoyed it, to be honest... Did you ever see 'Vanishing Point'? Like it's a part of art... like this Matrix thing is that this is all sort of a computer program. But it's noth-

349

ing new. It's all been said before. Sartre said it himself, y'know. Well, not as a computer program, obviously... but an experiment. Everything is an experiment..." *(Another pause.)* "But do you know what I'm getting at? D'ya understand what I'm saying?"

"I think so."

"I don't have any answers. I've only got the questions, y'know..."

"Don't you get a little, well, guarded around somebody who thinks they have all the answers?"

"I try to get the answers, but never do... and that's what makes it interesting. If you have the answers, wouldn't it all be boring? Like if you truly knew that this was all a test tube experiment on somebody's big table, or we all lived in the dust or the dirt of a fella's fingernail. If you knew that, y'know... people wouldn't be horticulturists, they'd all be anarchists. Hmm, it's an interesting image, isn't it? Anarchists and horticulturists..."

"So you write yourself, do you?"

"Some... not a lot. But over the years, I've enjoyed writing, keeping journals from adolescence up to the present. And written a few short articles. I hope to be doing more writing. But if this project comes to the point of being, or taking shape, let's say, to a book, I really am not going to be writing it. All of you who have thoughts and feelings to share, in essence you're the ones writing it. I'll be just putting the bits and pieces together."

"The jigsaw puzzle..."

(Long pause.)

"So you're a Sister, eh?"

"Yes..."

"People on the whole, they judge you on your stature, you know what I mean? I think it's very interesting. Like when I was doing the interviews for the local elections, I decided we wouldn't mention what their profession was. It was just their party and their name, with their name first, and the party next. But the party was in smaller lettering. It was all psychological, and it worked, because people weren't obsessed with the whole thing that he's a doctor, right, so we'll vote for him, y'know."

"This is the very reason why I am in secular clothes while here. One man who was ninety-two admitted he wasn't so sure how he felt about seeing a Sister not wearing a habit. He was OK with it, and we did a lot of joking. But after we were talking a while, he seemed quite comfortable and relaxed. 'Now, Jack, if I had been wearing a habit, would you have felt as free to say what you've said?' and he laughed and said 'no.' In the States, some people say they love to see the collar, they love to see the habit. And I often want to say, 'But how do you think we feel? We're on display all the time.' Wearing the 'outfit' also pushes some people's buttons. Any bitterness and anger at the Church gets directed at any of us wearing a habit or a collar."

"When we were in school, we had to wear uniforms, whatever, and there wasn't a week went by that I wasn't sent home to get a tie because my whole ideal was to not wear a tie and get in trouble, so I wouldn't be ruled to havin' to wear the uniform. At least I would wear the

jumper [*sweater*] and the shirt and the pants, but would-
n't wear the tie. And there was a whole group of us like
that who were at that. I know what you're saying…"

*"I've always been a bit of a maverick, even in the
community. It's amazing I got as far as I did. Sometimes
I wonder how they even elected me to Life Profession!
But they knew they needed fresh, new energy. They needed a transfusion, really… It must be the Irish blood in me
that gets that kind of spirit. It's almost a miracle that I'm
here at all, that they gave me permission to come over
here. But they know that they're not going to get any new
vocations—and this goes across the board, whether in
the States, Ireland, wherever—they cannot have an iron
fist. They cannot anymore try to break people's spirit
when they come in. They're going to have to just learn to
accept that, if they want new vocations. They have to
allow them to be, to be who they are. And it's the same
all around, whether you're going into a religious vocation or not. The Church has tried to suppress that kind of
free spirit. What I see—and I think some others as well—
what's happening is people are fed up, especially young
people, and they're saying, 'No more, I'm not going to
do it anymore.' Just like lots of things in history, the pen-*

353

dulum might swing to the extreme, but it will come back. And maybe there'll be a healing, and a reconciliation someday... and it will be a new Church."

"Would you be interested in Zen and Buddhism?"

"Very much so... It's in my background, before entering community."

"Have you, yeah? I'm fascinated by it, to be honest..."

"I'll tell you a little bit about myself..."

John and I continued to have a 'chat,' and I shared with him some of my life's story.

was it all a part of a grand design...

John asked if I was interested in Zen and Buddhism. Certainly at one time in my life I was, let's say, immersed in Zen... during the early 1980s. It was just after finishing a graduate degree in the field of Human Development. I became fascinated with Zen Buddhism, practicing zazen (sitting meditation, or contemplative prayer) on a regular basis. Zen is so present-centered, teaching us to be living in the moment... fully alive, fully aware. It's a great discipline. Once the seeds are sown, they grow and bear fruit for years to come.

I was born and grew up in New Jersey, not far from

355

New York City, the youngest of three daughters, which, of course, had its positives and negatives. My two older sisters nicknamed me "little Liz" (my middle name is Elizabeth) or "little brat," depending on their mood at any given moment! The two of them were close in age, with somewhat of a gap when their kid sister came along. I remember spending a lot of time alone, although there were lots of little friends nearby.

I didn't mind being alone, and actually liked it. Our family had a log cabin on a lake, nestled in a wooded area. It was really the size of a small house, with several rooms, running water, and a coal-burning stove. Summers were spent there, and I couldn't wait for the last day of school, knowing we were going up to "the lake" soon. One memory is the space of time after lunch. We (well, the three of us kids) were to have a whole hour of "quiet time." We couldn't play games during this period. Each of us had to find a place off by ourselves. We could read, take a nap, do crafts, whatever... In the early years, one favorite activity during the quiet hour was crayoning in coloring books. The front screened-in porch often provided that special place. The hour flew by! We kept the crayons in a round cookie tin, and to this day the scent of crayons is absolutely transporting, leading to another place, another dimension...

During the school year, our family first lived in a community with a network of sidewalks, designed so a child would never have to cross a street. Riding a small two-wheeled bike was another favorite pastime. A very special place was a hillside about a mile away, near the school. Once arriving there, the bike had to be walked into the tall grasses. Putting it down on its side, I would then quietly walk over to just the right spot, and lie on my back. Both the bike and I were lost in the grasses, totally removed from the world. It seemed hours would go by, yet it actually was possibly fifteen to twenty minutes. The clouds would totally occupy my attention, always changing, constantly moving. The fragrance of the grasses filled the air, and time seemed to stand still...

When I was about that same age (five years old), the family was given a Cocker Spaniel puppy named Cleo. In many ways, that dog was my best friend, always present and listening during the rough patches of my childhood and emotional adolescence.

I was a quiet kid and took life rather seriously, doing my homework when I was supposed to, and practicing the flute religiously. My first loves were music and tennis, but the flute finally eclipsed everything. I began taking private lessons with Paige Brook, a flutist with the New York Philharmonic. After five years of studying with him, I decided to go to Ithaca College in NY State. I wasn't ready.

This was the first taste of any kind of freedom away from home. Although the music students were dedicated, often shutting ourselves in tiny practice rooms for hours in a day, we also spent some time downtown with our pitchers of beer! Needless to say, I flunked a few courses, which was not acceptable to my father. I'll never forget, while having dinner with my family on New Year's Eve in a fancy restaurant overlooking the NY skyline, my dad asked, "Have you thought about what you will be doing now? I am not paying for any more of your education." On the one hand, it was a shock, but on the other, I knew it was coming. Looking back now, it was the best thing he could have done. Tough love, isn't that what they call it?

Yet I persevered, because when you have music in your blood you cannot possibly ignore the inner promptings. I had the opportunity to study with Joseph Mariano (Eastman School of Music.) Mr. Mariano was one of the most sought after teachers at the time.

With his encouragement, I ended up getting my first

"gig" in my short-lived career as a professional flutist. These "gigs" or jobs were nothing less than an experience out of a novel! On two sides of a spectrum, the experience was considered either "training" for the young up-and-coming stars in the music world or, in essence, being put out to pasture for the "has-beens." Some of these veterans were well into their seventies, having performed under giants like Bruno Walter and Toscanini. We'd be on the road for weeks at a time, with people dropping out like flies with heart attacks, kidney infections, or pneumonia. I'll never forget one conductor who, on the very first night of the tour (after we had signed our contracts), informed us that he saw himself as an animal trainer, and we were his dogs...

There were a few more orchestra jobs after that. After several years of playing in small minor league orchestras and chamber groups, it became quite clear that this was not how I wanted to spend the rest of my life. The flute was in many ways my soul, yet most of the big-league orchestras were not hiring women at that time. Female instrumentalists could rarely ever "make it" very far. Actually, the future appeared rather bleak. So that was the end of my dream to be a professional flutist! I returned to New Jersey and finished a degree in

Fine Arts and Psychology, working as an artist for a small textile engraving firm. I continued to perform locally with a harpsichordist, as well as give individual flute instruction on the side. Doing very well academically, I went on for a graduate degree in Human Development, but not without some scholarship aid and loans. Where all this was leading was very much in question, but somehow I knew it would all come together someday.

By now surely some of you are wondering if marriage was ever in the picture! The usual response is, "Well, I never actually signed the papers, or walked down the aisle..." It was a very full life, with numerous affairs and relationships. I seemed to have this propensity for falling in love with the wrong men! But looking back, I can't help but wonder, was it all a part of a grand design...

And why is an Episcopal nun from the States writing a book about Ireland? Well, it's on my Mom's side of the family where you find the Irish ancestry, from County Cork and Galway. I was baptized in Queen of All Saints RC Church in Brooklyn, New York, brought up a Quaker, and am now an Episcopal Sister.

Over the years, our Mom would tell us stories about our Irish relatives. But it wasn't until a first trip to

Ireland, in 1986, when the realization hit me of how strong the connection truly was. While there, after a few days the strangest feeling came over me that I had been there before—a feeling of "coming home," not unlike most individuals when they are on a journey to search out their roots. Ten years passed before it was possible to return. Then, in 1999, I began taking small groups to Ireland each spring (already living in community, this was one way of getting back to that enchanted land!)

There is an Irish or Scottish poem that is a favorite for many of us. Apparently the origins are from an ancient Gaelic blessing, yet it might have been written yesterday. It seems appropriate to share it...

> May the blessings of light be on you, light
> without and light within.
>
> May the blessed sunshine shine on you and
> warm your heart until it glows like a great
> peat fire, so that the stranger may come and
> warm himself,
> and also a friend.

361

And may the light shine out of the two eyes of
you, like a candle set in two windows of a
house, bidding the wanderer to
come in out of the storm...

May the blessing of the Rain be on you, the
soft, sweet rain. May it fall upon your spirit,
so that all the flowers may spring up, and shed
their sweetness on the air.

And may the blessing of the Great Rains be on
you. May they beat upon your spirit and wash
it fair and clean and leave there many a shin-
ing pool, where the blue heaven shines reflected,
and sometimes a star...

And may the blessing of the Earth be on you,
the great round earth.

May it be soft under you when you lie out
upon it, tired at the end of the day.

And may the earth rest easily over you, when
at last you be out under it.

May it rest so lightly over you that your soul
may be quickly through it,
and up, and off... and on its way to God.

Lovely, isn't it? The title for the book just seemed to spring from the poem. We all need to remember to be open and aware to receive God's blessings that are showered on us every day. And so many of the themes in the poem can still be seen and felt in Ireland, Scotland, Wales, Cornwall... the warm hospitality offered to strangers, the light in their faces, the closeness to the earth, the awareness of the changes in the weather.

And where do I find God? What sustains me? It's always been through nature... the sound of a rippling stream, birds chattering in the spring, a gentle rain... quality of light, sparkles on water, clouds... the fragrance of the air after a storm in the summer, the sweet smell of a peat fire... stillness. Seeking the "Holy," trying to find whatever it is that transcends the ordinary, making every effort to encourage others to do the same. Living in community can get monotonous, regardless of the built-in structure of prayer and worship. We often forget the "bigger picture," getting too caught up with unimportant "stuff." Yes, even those of us living a so-called holy life can be derailed...

None of us is perfect. Everyone makes mistakes. But somehow we all need to work together to try to build a better world. The walls that separate and divide must crumble; our denominational and cultural boundaries must become porous, like a living, breathing organism. We need to be willing to learn from one another, putting aside our differences as well as our prejudices. We need to live, and *love*, as if each and every action will make a difference... we need to believe this with every fiber of our existence.

What sustains you? Where do you find God? Are you at peace with yourself, with others, with God? Isn't there a longing in all of us for peace, both inwardly and outwardly? It is so empowering when the realization occurs for each of us that we have choices, throughout any given day. We may not be aware of it, but we choose what is life-giving, or what is life-denying, every moment of our existence. We can choose whatever it is that leads toward health, toward a sense of well-being, toward peace of mind. Or we can choose that which is life-denying, leading inevitably to our own demise.

We can choose to live in the past, in fear, anger, and bitterness, trapped in our own self-imposed prisons. Or we can choose to live in the present, with optimism and hope, looking forward to a better future. One way leads down a spiral path to hell... The other leads to life, and toward God.

"I have set before you life and death,
     blessing and curse;
Therefore choose life,
that you and your descendants may live"

— Deuteronomy 30:19.

For God's sake, choose life...

SOMETIMES A STAR...

About the Author

M.E. Colman is a life-professed member of the Convent of St. John Baptist, an Episcopal religious community for women in Mendham, NJ. Before becoming a nun, Sister Margo had a varied background in music, art, and psychology. After completing undergraduate work in Fine Arts and Psychology, she earned a M.A. degree in Human Development from Farleigh Dickinson University.

Interest in the spiritual side of human nature has always been an integral part of Sister Margo's life, from childhood to the present. In 1983-84, she attended Pendle Hill, a Quaker center for study and contemplation in Wallingford, PA. While there, she had the chance to meet and get to know many gifted individuals in the area of spiritual growth, some of whom filled the roles of mentor, guide, and friend. Among them were Douglas Steere, Parker Palmer, Sandra Cronk, Donald Swann, and John Yungblut. A few years later, she took part in a ten-day Intensive in Centering Prayer with Thomas Keating.

Sister Margo is currently in charge of St. Marguerite's, the community's retreat and conference center. She also has years of experience in doing spiritual direction, often using her training in psychology and Ignatian Spirituality.

Another very important facet in M.E. Colman's life is leading groups to Ireland, Scotland, Wales and Cornwall. These truly enchanted lands are so richly endowed with legends and folklore from the past, yet also providing the opportunity to meet and experience the people and their culture as they are today.